MW01491201

.

THE RIGHT SIDE OF HAPPINESS

A Practical Guide For Embracing
Mindfulness And Living Your Best Life

THE RIGHT SIDE OF HAPPINESS

A Practical Guide For Embracing
Mindfulness And Living Your Best Life

ANNAMARIE FERNYAK

ethos
collective

THE RIGHT SIDE OF HAPPINESS
© 2024 by Annamarie Fernyak. All rights reserved.

Printed in the United States of America

Published by Igniting Souls
PO Box 43, Powell, OH 43065
IgnitingSouls.com

LCCN: 2024921292
Paperback ISBN: 978-1-63680-413-2
Hardcover ISBN: 978-1-63680-414-9
e-book ISBN: 978-1-63680-415-6

Available in paperback, hardcover, e-book, and audiobook.

Any Internet addresses (websites, blogs, etc.) and telephone numbers printed in this book are offered as a resource. They are not intended in any way to be or imply an endorsement by Igniting Souls, nor does Igniting Souls vouch for the content of these sites and numbers for the life of this book.

Some names and identifying details may have been changed to protect the privacy of individuals.

Table of Contents

Introduction

We are living in an era of unprecedented technological growth. As someone who attended high school when typing classes were still a thing and later weathered the Y2K hysteria, I never could have imagined a world of smartphones, artificial intelligence, and gene splicing. Today, most of us are living longer than our ancestors, and if metrics such as education, disease prevention, and physical possessions are any indication, our collective quality of life is better than it's ever been. Nevertheless, so many of us struggle to feel truly happy.

Why?

I've spent the better part of my career exploring the answers to this question. As a certified life coach and mindfulness meditation teacher, I've helped lots of individuals find meaning, purpose, and even happiness. I've seen firsthand the benefits of a consistent mindfulness practice, as well as the struggles people of all ages encounter when they don't establish a foundation for self-reflection, present moment awareness, and the ability to shift their mindset—all very achievable results from practicing mindfulness.

Possibly you've already seen the hype around mindfulness and its impacts, and you may be questioning if the mere act of paying attention can really change your life. That skepticism is totally understandable. It seems like every week, new articles appear demonstrating how mindfulness can help with everything from work productivity and classroom performance to postpartum depression and a couple's sex life.

There's plenty of hard science to back up these claims, and I doubt you'd be able to find a doctor, psychologist, or religious leader who advocates *against* the benefits of a mindfulness practice. However, most of us struggle to make it a tangible part of our daily lives. That's at least in part because our culture's hard-won prosperity has left many of us feeling overburdened, saturated with information, and just plain overwhelmed. We may understand the benefits of a mindfulness practice, but who has time to convert their closet into a Pinterest-worthy meditation nook or sit on a cushion for an hour a day?

Not me, that's for sure. And probably not you, either.

But here's the good news: You don't have to.

The Right Side of Happiness is a no-nonsense guide to incorporating mindfulness into your daily life. I first began working on this book after witnessing many motivated people either give up on their mindfulness practice or talk themselves out of even beginning.

Many of my new clients have told me they feel daunted or even intimidated by the concept of mindfulness. I imagine that's because they picture days spent in silent retreat at an austere zendo temple or a month-long residency at an Indian Ashram. I'm all for both experiences, but neither really fits into my lifestyle. Although I may be the founder and CEO of a successful mindfulness education firm, the reality of my schedule is I'm lucky to squeeze in fifteen minutes of formal meditation on any given day. My guess is you feel the same way.

But don't let that daunt you. The great news is science has proven again and again that those fifteen minutes—or ten minutes, or five minutes—are more than enough to start seeing real benefits in mental concentration and an overall sense of well-being. Better yet, opportunities for practical mindfulness are everywhere. Oftentimes, these opportunities arise in the most mundane and unexpected places, whether it's while driving, sitting through a tedious Zoom call, or interacting with the people we love. And that's even more great news because those situations are often where we most *need* the benefits of mindfulness.

My current breakfast situation is a great example. I've always been susceptible to interior mental dialogues about the choices I make, whether it's what to wear, whether or not to exercise, or even what and when I decide to eat. About a year ago, I was diagnosed with high cholesterol, and my doctor made it very clear I needed to change my diet. This was particularly bad news for someone who not only loves food, but who has also spent most of her life thinking she can solve life's major problems by eating a wedge of cheese.

I know the best breakfast choice for me is oatmeal with berries: not only will the whole grains lower my cholesterol, but the fruit provides the healthful antioxidants and fiber I need. Together, they also work to prevent those nagging junk food cravings later in the day.

The problem is that most days what I really want is a decadent piece of avocado toast topped with a fried egg and a drizzle of pesto. That's especially true if I'm tired or overwhelmed (rich, savory food has always been an emotional comfort for me). Some mornings, I might also crave a peanut butter sandwich, not realizing the sugar and fat are actually a Hail Mary attempt to stave off nausea from an oncoming migraine.

I can't begin to count the number of times I've begun my day standing at my kitchen refrigerator, agonizing over these choices and rationalizing my way out of a bowl of oatmeal. Altogether, I'm sure it's been hours—precious time I could have dedicated to work or hobbies or the people I love.

You may have a similar story, whether it's about an internal debate concerning your parenting choices, your tendency to binge-watch TV, or a habit of doom-scrolling through social media. Perhaps you're trying to limit your sugar, alcohol, or nicotine intake and have had mixed results. Regardless of the source of this internal dialogue, practical mindfulness can help.

Mindfulness allows us to interrupt our old, habituated narratives. It allows us to put our brain on notice, to take back control of our decision-making, and to live a more intentional and purpose-driven life. In *The Right Side of Happiness*, we'll not only explore the science behind how and why this practice works, but also the very real ways you can begin incorporating it into your routine.

As you'll see in subsequent chapters, this book is primarily about evolving your mindset and determining what practices you can incorporate into your life and routines. Every time you add a little mindfulness to your present experience, you're taking a very big step forward on the path toward leading to your best life.

To aid your journey, *The Right Side of Happiness* provides both formal and informal mindfulness exercises that help you identify and live your goals and values. You may benefit from incorporating some of these exercises directly into your daily practice. Others, you may choose to modify or disregard. That's all okay. What's important is you choose what feels right to you.

More than anything, *The Right Side of Happiness* is intended to help you discover your own approach to being mindful. Along the way, we'll explore the powerful connections between body and mind and how that interplay informs everything, from what we do with stress and trauma to our ability to tap into our own internal wisdom and capacity for self-love.

Will mindfulness make your life perfect? Definitely not. But it will allow you to embrace imperfections and find happiness despite and *because* of them. Take my great love of cheese, which you'll read more about in the coming pages. I have a lot of emotional baggage and old habits associated with this love. Ever since I was a child, cheese has been my go-to comfort food, and I've accumulated a lifetime of guilt and shame associated with this habit.

As you'll soon come to learn, I can also be a pro at unhelpful judgment, both about myself and other people. Left to my own devices, I can find myself in a toxic cycle of unexamined habits and self-recriminations when presented with something as simple as an individually wrapped mozzarella stick. No matter how much I may love a good piece of cheese, there's no joy in eating it and then feeling bad about it later.

Mindfulness breaks this emotional food loop. By being fully present, I can truly enjoy those moments when I treat myself to some great artisanal Swiss cheese made by a local creamery not far from my house. And when I do, I'm even more aware of the pleasure that experience has to offer. As far as I'm concerned, that's what real happiness is all about.

As for my breakfast conundrum? When approached from a place of mindfulness, I have found there are actually multiple opportunities for me to reroute the internal debate—or even to put an end to it entirely. This process can begin with something as simple as opening the refrigerator door.

That little blast of cold air touching my skin and face is like a bell, reminding me to pause and notice what's happening in my body: What physical sensations can I observe? Do I, for instance, notice signs of stress in my neck, shoulders, or belly? That same rush of cold air is also a cue to think about what external influences might be at play in my cravings: Did I get enough sleep? What's on tap for me at work today, and how might that be influencing my mood?

In just the few seconds required for me to take stock of what's happening in my mind and body, I'm engaging with my mindfulness practice and amassing important information that will help me make decisions that align with my goals and values. By taking the time to observe and notice the present moment, I can also ascertain what's behind my desire for a quick shot of sugar or fat and decide if that's really the best choice for me at that moment.

Additionally, pausing for a moment to pay attention to what's happening in our bodies and brains allows us to lean into self-compassion. Those few seconds are just enough time to remind us what neuroscience has to say about the challenges we all face when working to change a habit.

As we'll explore in more detail throughout this book, the human brain is a complex system of regions and structures that regulate every aspect of our behavior, from our feelings and memories to our decision-making skills. Nevertheless, it doesn't always have our best interest at heart.

Throughout *The Right Side of Happiness*, I'll offer you techniques and tools to strengthen willpower, to make more conscious choices, and to tap into your immense reservoir of intuition and emotional intelligence. Along the way, I'll demonstrate the ways that a mindfulness practice doesn't just allow you to be more present, but how it also encourages us to cultivate greater honesty and vulnerability. Not only do these benefits allow us to radically improve our own well-being, but they allow us to improve every aspect of our lives, from our careers to our most cherished relationships.

Will mindfulness make your life perfect?

Mmmmm, no. But it will allow you to embrace imperfections and find happiness despite (and even because of) them. No matter what interior monologue or life experience brought you to this book, practical mindfulness can offer the same meaning and joy to your life as well. With very little effort, you'll soon find your daily routine offers countless opportunities for greater awareness and self-growth.

To get started, all you have to do is turn the page.

··· | ···
An Introduction to Mindfulness

MY HUSBAND AND I love every opportunity to retreat to a small lake house we purchased several years ago. Something about that space always relaxes and inspires me. Even the bathroom seems built for peaceful contemplation, with its high ceilings, hardwood floors, and a quirky oversized vanity that's built on two chunky, ornately carved, piano legs.

However, these days it's what is perched on that vanity that really stands out to me: a picture frame, gifted to me by one of my oldest childhood friends. Together, we're the quintessential odd couple: she's an extrovert who lives her life in multicolor; I'm an introvert who prefers to wear the same black shirt and skirt every day. She is 5'10" tall, blond, and built like Marilyn Monroe, while I am 5'2" with graying hair and a decidedly less alluring figure. Those differences may be one reason we've been best friends since sixth grade. They also mean we sometimes see each other better than we see ourselves.

A few years ago, my friend purchased this picture frame as a present, no doubt thinking I would adore it (gifts are her love language). But even knowing it came from someone I cherish wasn't enough for me to love this gift. The frame itself is a wash of coral, turquoise, and emerald, all swirled together—far more Bohemian than my usual decorating style. Amidst all those swirls, the frame features the face of a serene looking woman. Near her, in what looks like letters torn from a journal page, is printed one word: *Seeker*.

That word alone led me to promptly take my friend's very thoughtful gift and stash it deep inside a closet. I'm sure she meant "seeker" as a compliment—a way of saying she appreciated something about the way I live my life. But that word, printed so boldly on the frame, felt like an allegation.

Seeking was the last way I wanted to spend my time. To me, the idea of being a seeker inherently implies you're always in a state of searching and never quite finding the object of your search. It's about restlessness and striving.

I know there is a time when it's beneficial to embrace that kind of search. In fact, I spent a good part of my adult life in such a state: passionately searching for what, specifically, I don't think I even knew. Enlightenment, maybe. Some kind of transformation, certainly. However, at some point along my evolution, I realized if I identified myself as a seeker, then that is what I'd always be doing—searching, rather than finding.

Around the time of that revelation, I'd also begun my own mindfulness practice. I was beginning to see the real benefits of paying conscious attention to the present moment, and that practice felt antithetical to seeking.

Instead, I'd come to realize mindfulness is about meta-phorically setting up camp wherever you happen to be. It's about exploring everything that's happening in the here and now, and allowing everything you discover in *this* moment to be the foundation for the next one. When I began to experience the reservoir of inner wisdom that was always available to me, I stopped my ceaseless seeking. In time, I abandoned that part of my identity altogether. And that's when I truly became comfortable in my own skin.

My mindfulness path has definitely been a journey—and one with more than a few bumpy spots. Some days are easier than others. I still lose my temper with slow drivers and sometimes even with my very supportive husband, who walks this path with me. But that's okay, the important thing is I'm happy with who I am. I am living, and continuing to grow into, my best life.

As for that picture frame? I finally realized hiding it deep in a closet wasn't going to exorcize my seeking tendencies. I'd also come to understand that keeping opportunities for improvement in my peripheral vision isn't just an avenue for growth; it's a form of seeking I can actually embrace.

So after some soul-searching, I pulled that frame out of the closet and found the perfect photo to display inside: a picture of four of my beautiful nieces.

At the time, they spanned in age from six to almost thirteen. The photo captures them standing in a little huddle with their arms wrapped around each other, and one of them is looking directly at the camera with the biggest Cheshire cat grin on her face. You can tell she's up to something—almost as if she's challenging the person taking the picture. More importantly, you can tell she, her sister, and her two cousins are living in the present moment and having the best time.

There's something about that combination of being fully present, their exuberant connection, and my niece with her air of defiance that negates the concept of "seeking" in all the right ways. Now, whenever I walk into our lake house bathroom and see that photo and frame, I can't help but smile.

True gifts sometimes take time to be realized.

The Gift of the Present

Google "mindfulness" and you'll find nearly as many definitions as there are teachers and practitioners. Some focus on the science of the brain; others tie the practice to organized religions or a spiritual tradition. Still others are so obscure they sound like they were written by a medieval mystic or guru who spent his life living alone on a remote mountain top.

For some new or potential students of mindfulness, this cacophony of definitions and approaches undoubtedly leads to confusion, reluctance, or beliefs that the practice is inaccessible and complex.

When it comes to conceptualizing mindfulness in my own life and teaching, I like the simple clarity of a definition offered by Jon Kabat-Zinn. An emeritus professor at the University of Massachusetts Medical School, Kabat-Zinn founded that university's Center for Mindfulness and went on to author several well-respected books written for a lay audience.

Widely considered one of the leading experts on the subject, Kabat-Zinn defines mindfulness this way: "awareness that arises through paying attention, on purpose, in the present moment, non-judgmentally."[1] That's it. By choosing to consciously pay attention to the present, and doing so without judging what arises, we are not only practicing mindfulness, we are also gaining more understanding about ourselves and the worlds we occupy.

In my years as a mindfulness teacher, I've heard a lot of misconceptions about the practice. Some of my new clients tell me they expect to find a silent room filled with "perfect" meditators, all perched on cushions in an effortless lotus position.

Others tell me they picture happy-go-lucky yoga instructors gracefully hopping from cloud to cloud while sipping kale juice, chanting, and ringing bells. They worry that a mindfulness practice will require them to be fully present around the clock, or that they'll be expected to maintain a constant state of empty-headed bliss.

Thankfully, mindfulness requires none of that (though I do love a good green smoothie). Mindfulness can be practiced in many positions and even while in motion. It's as powerful when we're agitated or even downright angry as it is when we're attempting to find nirvana. I've discovered through my own experience that you can practice mindfulness while brushing your teeth, taking out the garbage, and waiting in line at the grocery store or DMV.

Mindfulness is not necessarily synonymous with meditation (we'll talk more about that later in the chapter), nor does it need to be tied to any kind of spiritual pursuit. Instead, living mindfully is simply a state of mind that can become a part of any moment in your day.

Mindfulness is also not an organized religion. In fact, in my role as a mindfulness coach for professional organizations and as a mindfulness curriculum content editor for public school educators, I've intentionally kept mindfulness a secular practice for the workplace, teachers, and elementary school students I encounter.

In school classrooms, for instance, we define mindfulness as "paying attention to what's happening right here and right now." It's a simple concept that can be easily understood by both teachers and students. After a few times practicing together, even the littles begin to catch on and repeat alongside the teacher, "Right here, right now."

When we embrace the present moment without judgment or complaint, we can also begin to remove the filters of habits, beliefs, and memories of past experiences that cloud and distort our perceptions. In place of all those crutches, we can be curious; we can explore with an open mind and allow for the possibility of seeing and experiencing the world around us from a new viewpoint. We also come to realize that the wisdom we need already resides within us.

If you happen to be a spiritual or religious person, this practice can enhance your spirituality and allow you to connect with your religion in a deeper, more embodied way. Mindfulness can also help you become truly present to your religion's teachings and how best to incorporate them into your life.

Even if you do not subscribe to a particular theology or spirituality, mindfulness is just as helpful at enhancing your life in a secular world. Why? Because at its core, mindfulness is a way of living that asks us to pay attention with intent. It provides the tools we need to regulate our attention and sometimes even our emotions. It allows us to see ourselves and the world around us from different perspectives.

In other words, it provides all the information we need to make conscious choices that support us in living our best life.

Mindfulness is also proven to work. Decades of scientific studies point to the physical, emotional, and psychological benefits of the practice. For instance, in 2020 a group of mindfulness scholars conducted an extensive study of academic and scholarly publications dedicated to the benefits of mindfulness.

They found dozens of research-based articles proving that mindfulness not only improves our overall well-being, but can also be used to treat everything from depression to chronic pain. Used in conjunction with other treatments, mindfulness minimizes harmful symptoms associated with psychosis, addiction, PTSD, and diseases like cancer and multiple sclerosis.[2]

Mindfulness also offers other, slightly less tangible benefits as well. It encourages a gradual process of learning to trust in oneself and our own inherent gifts and powers. It's a recognition that a light already resides in all of us. Mindfulness is the act of pulling off the lampshade so that your light can shine brightly in any room.

This doesn't happen immediately, of course. It takes practice and time to build confidence, to understand the unique language of your mind and body, and to learn how to see yourself and the world around you without the filters of your habits, beliefs, and memories of past experiences.

Mindfulness also requires that we learn compassion for ourselves and others. In return, mindfulness builds empathy and reveals to us our true humanness. It also shows us the parts of ourselves that we share with our family and friends, co-workers, and supervisors: the psychology, physiology, and instinctual behaviors I like to think of as *the human condition.*

Through our mindfulness practice, we gradually begin to understand how we are affected and influenced by the world around us, and how we, in turn, inspire the world. We learn to recognize our triggers, along with the guilt and shame they can produce. We also gain greater recognition of how *others* are triggered and how this can impact us. Doing so frees us from the shackles of mindless assumptions, expectations, and the court of public opinion. It creates a path toward true freedom.

Making the Commitment

In his book, *A New Earth: Awakening to Your Life's Purpose,* the great mindfulness teacher and best-selling author Eckhart Tolle tells the story of his own path to enlightenment. As he explains it, Tolle initially felt a superiority and satisfaction after he dedicated himself to a life of study and quiet contemplation. In an effort to embody the values of that kind of life, Tolle also traded in his fancy car for a bicycle. One day, he found himself riding his bike alongside a Mercedes.

"Look at me," he told the driver. "I traded my gas guzzling car for an efficient, ecologically sound bicycle. I'm more present than you."

Tolle continued to congratulate himself with thoughts of how much more enlightened he was because of the humble path he'd taken. Then, to his surprise, the driver responded, "No, you're not, Idiot. Your ego's still in the way. You think you're superior simply because you're riding a bicycle, but the fact is that your ego is making you less again."

That anecdote has always stuck with me. As you'll see throughout this book, I, like most humans, can get judgmental when left to my own devices and conditioning. From time to time, I need to be reminded of the societal norms and prejudices that have created class distinctions, along with the assumptions and biases they can provoke within me.

Mindfulness is the perfect tool to help us become aware when we are making such assumptions or judgments. It provides tools that allow us to notice the human condition—those unconscious characteristics and limitations of life that are shared by all of us—and what that condition looks like as it plays out in any given moment. Through mindfulness, we can sit and merely observe all of this, rather than having to make sense of it, categorize it, or criticize ourselves and others.

For some people, making the choice to live a mindful life can feel intimidating or downright scary. Mindfulness and meditation both require an element of trusting you are safe to let go and be in the moment. Many of us are conditioned to fear what happens when we let our minds go, when we begin to pay attention to our thoughts, or when we allow ourselves to fully feel the sensations of our body and emotions.

In my experience, this is particularly true for people who subscribe to religions that include a strong emphasis on the power of the devil. Growing up Catholic, I was raised to believe letting go of judgments and encouraging my mind into a state of stillness could open me up to temptation from evil. Some of my clients tell me they were raised in faiths that encouraged similar beliefs. For them, being present comes with the additional challenge of establishing new beliefs.

The trust and openness mindfulness requires can feel especially challenging for people who have experienced profound trauma in their lives. For these individuals, the prospect (and process) of relaxing control of the mind and paying attention to sensations and experiences is psychologically terrifying.

If that sounds familiar to you, you may want to consider beginning your mindfulness journey with the assistance of a mental health professional, someone who shares your principles and faith, or possibly with a group of people who relate to your experiences—people you trust to create and maintain a feeling of personal safety.

Because mindfulness is a commitment to being present with what is happening in the moment, we must learn to sit with uncomfortable emotions. While we may not love the prospect of doing so, mindfulness nevertheless asks us to sit with the full range of human emotions—and not all of them are a lot of fun. However, they are an undeniable part of the human experience.

Even the most highly trained mindfulness teachers still experience grief, sadness, anger, and other challenging emotions. The difference is they've learned the skills to work through these emotions in a productive way.

Mindfulness can provide those skills for you, too. It can allow the time and foster the tools needed to acknowledge your emotions from a safe distance without forcing you to feel consumed by them.

An ability to create distance between you and these challenging emotions allows you to make a conscious choice about what you want to do with those feelings: by establishing a perimeter of space around them, you empower yourself to approach those feelings with clarity and a bit of detachment. In that regard, it's almost like you become an empathetic friend to yourself—someone who hears and understands how you are feeling, but also has the distance and strength needed to support you or offer counsel.

After spending some time developing your own mindfulness practice, you'll learn to watch feelings float by like clouds in the sky. You'll have the wherewithal to make conscious choices about which emotions you want to let go by, and which emotions you want to dedicate your body, mind, and spirit to confronting or processing. You'll learn compassion for yourself and empathy for others. You'll come to understand your own needs, gifts, and limitations, and how to set boundaries that honor them.

If arriving at such a state sounds impossible or like a daunting amount of work, fear not. One of the best aspects of a mindful life is how simple it is to begin incorporating the tenets of mindfulness into your life. The trick is simply in noticing: taking time each day to observe how you're feeling and what your mind and body are telling you.

For instance, as you stand in the grocery store line after a busy day of work, how do your feet feel inside your shoes? What does the plastic bar on the shopping cart feel like in your hands? When a driver cuts you off in traffic or drives ten miles below the speed limit, where do you feel the resulting emotion in your body? Is it a tightness in your chest? A red fog that momentarily takes over your brain? The more time you can give to these quick little moments of awareness, the more advanced your mindfulness practice will become.

And don't worry: like all other worthwhile pursuits, mindfulness requires practice. It's a skill much like learning to play pickleball or painting with watercolors. Gradually over time, our bodies, minds, and hearts become habituated to the practice, and it becomes much easier—almost automatic.

As you'll see throughout this book, there are easy tricks and tools to make mindfulness a part of even the busiest day, such as setting alarms on your smartphone. I find the tinkle of that alert is all it takes for me to stop and spend a few seconds feeling my breath or observing the sensations in my body. And I think you'll be pleasantly surprised to see what a difference those little moments of awareness can make.

Another great aspect of a mindfulness practice is it's yours to personalize and make your own. Although this book offers lots of great informal and formal practices, you get to choose what works best for you.

For instance, a friend of mine once told me about his own approach to a daily mindfulness practice. At the time, he worked in a toxic office situation where he and his supervisor did not get along. She could be very aggressive and unprofessional, and initially her behavior would send my friend spinning.

One day, that supervisor called my friend into her office. As he got up from behind his desk, he felt an immediate sense of dread. He'd already made up his mind that whatever was about to happen would be unpleasant.

Then, just outside her door, he decided to try a mindfulness exercise. He stood in *tadasana*, or mountain pose—the yoga stance where you stand with your feet parallel and hips-width apart, a neutral spine, and your arms at your sides, palms facing forward. Yogis believe *tadasana* is a stabilizing pose that fosters inner stability and peace, since it aligns our posture and helps to release the stress we tend to carry in our shoulders and necks.

Knowing the benefits of this pose, my friend took the opportunity to stand in *tadasana* while he took a few breaths and focused on the grounding sensation of his feet on the floor. Then he moved his awareness slowly up his body, noticing how his calves, knees, thighs, and the rest of his body felt in space.

He gently aligned his spine, correcting his posture by moving his shoulders back and down toward his hips, and continued to move his awareness upwards. When he made his way to the top of his head, he invited his entire body to relax. Then, he took a deep, conscious breath before opening his supervisor's door.

As soon as he walked inside, he could immediately tell the energy was different. Their subsequent encounter was remarkably pleasant, and he walked away knowing this positive encounter was influenced in no small part because *he* brought a different version of himself into her office.

One of the reasons I so appreciate that anecdote is because my friend chose to become an active participant in his subsequent interaction with his boss. Instead of merely responding to the energy and tone of the encounter, he worked to make it more positive and productive. We all have that ability.

A Word on Meditation

I mentioned earlier that mindfulness and meditation need not be synonymous. That said, mindfulness meditation can be an exercise that strengthens the ability to be mindful during everyday experiences.

Some readers might find meditation a useful way into their own mindfulness practice, especially if they already have a religious background. So many of the religions of the world include a form of meditation, whether it's prayer, saying the rosary, chanting a mantra, or using mala beads.

What all of these practices share in common is their ability to focus the attention of the participant and to move our riotous minds back to our present experience. One of my favorite forms of meditation is *Sufi dance*, where participants whirl and whirl until they've abandoned all other thoughts and concerns. Their minds are forced to focus on the movement of their feet, arms, and body in space, or they will crash into each other, tangle in their skirts, or fall over their own feet.

Zen Buddhists often practice a less robust but nevertheless physical form of *walking meditation*. The act of being deeply aware of the mechanics of your body as you lift first one foot, then your leg, followed by the other, can be a great way to focus attention, especially if you tend to feel a little fidgety with sedentary activities.

Some people find *guided meditation* to be a useful entry into the world of mindfulness. In the past few years, a remarkable number of smart device apps have appeared to facilitate this process. Some offer spoken instruction to provide guidance and help new meditators feel more confident. Others include timers or notifications that make scheduling meditation time much easier.

Regardless of what path you choose, know your meditation practice can be highly individualistic and tailored to your own needs and goals. Secular mindfulness practice encourages the freedom to explore the path that resonates with you. It can support you in evolving as a person so you can be your best, most present self.

Setting Yourself Up to Succeed

If you come to mindfulness hoping it will always bring you a sense of calm and peace, you're bound to be disappointed, as I once was. These experiences are best considered a welcome byproduct of a regular mindfulness practice. When my team works with educators, we emphasize the fact that mindfulness is a crucial piece, and often the missing *peace*, of social and emotional learning in the school curriculum.

Mindfulness doesn't teach kids how to avoid being angry or sad, but, instead, what to do when they experience those emotions. It provides the tools they need to identify what emotions look and feel like in their bodies, how to observe those emotions, and what to do when they experience them. It teaches them how to communicate their experiences and how to be compassionate when others are communicating theirs. It reminds them to take a deep breath before they say something they regret, and to speak honestly about how they feel.

When I talk about mindfulness being the missing piece/ peace, what I mean is mindfulness is a process that helps us to make our best choices, to evolve the habits and beliefs that may no longer be serving us, and to accurately identify feelings as they occur in our minds and bodies.

All of these benefits are the foundation for making lasting, positive changes in your life. The ability to accurately identify things happening in the world is the foundation for making lasting changes in your life. As the German management scholar Peter Drucker once said, "You can't manage what you can't measure."

Mindfulness will help you build the mental muscles needed to pay attention, shift your mindset, and make conscious choices. Prioritizing self-care through a consistent mindfulness meditation practice that aligns your mind and body will give you the fortitude and strength needed to engage those muscles during your day.

Of course, being present in the moment and with a deep awareness of what's actually happening can become a very sensual experience, and many people find that their senses become heightened, and the world around them seems vivid and intense. Sometimes, that experience can feel overwhelming, which is one reason it's impossible to practice mindfulness all the time. I imagine even the Dalai Lama feels frustrated and overwhelmed at times.

The difference between him and many of us is that a lifetime of mindfulness practice has taught him how to recognize those states early and practice the self-care he needs to get through them.

Chapter 1 Takeaways

- Mindfulness can be defined as *choosing to consciously pay attention to the present moment, and to do so without judging what arises.*

- Mindfulness does not have to be a part of a spiritual practice or organized religion.

- Research has shown that mindfulness benefits our physical, emotional, and psychological selves.

- One reason why mindfulness is beneficial is because it removes the filters of habits, beliefs, and memories, which can cloud and distort our perceptions. Mindfulness encourages us to explore the world with an open mind and to embrace the wisdom that already resides within us.

- Mindfulness can be practiced any time, anywhere. All it requires is for us to take the time to observe what our minds and bodies have to say in a given moment.

- Mindfulness and meditation need not be synonymous, but some people find meditation to be a useful way to begin their mindfulness journeys.

- Although mindfulness offers myriad benefits, some people may be best served undertaking it with the help of a trained psychological or medical professional. That can be especially true for people who have experienced profound trauma.

- Regardless of your past experience, your mindfulness practice will be most successful if you prioritize self-care to build willpower and make space for your newfound awareness.

Chapter 1 Exercises

Formal Mindfulness Practice

Setting Up Your Formal Mindfulness Meditation Practice

Throughout this book, I'll provide both formal and informal mindfulness exercises for you to try. Although I'm a firm believer in the power of informal mindfulness, I also believe there are myriad benefits associated with a more formal practice.

One main benefit is it develops our ability to observe thoughts in real time. Cultivating the ability to observe our thoughts, judgments, sensations, and emotions, as well as stimuli coming in from the world around us, allows us to make better, more informed decisions before we act.

Formal meditation also fosters our ability to notice habits and beliefs that are no longer supporting us. I personally have also noticed the way it decreases the number of times I experience shame or regret because of something I said or did (and later wished I hadn't). It also has allowed me to move beyond habituated narratives in my head that make me less likely to speak up, for fear that what I have to contribute may not be valid.

Of course, we're all human, and no amount of formal meditation will ensure we are able to move past unhelpful habits entirely. However, in my experience, this practice has helped me practice self-compassion in those moments and gently pull aside my pride and say, "I'm sorry."

Taking the time to establish a regular formal meditation practice can be a real boon to any mindfulness pursuit. What follows are some helpful tips to get you started.

1. **Find a comfortable place where you are safe and can relax.** In mindfulness meditation, the formal practice is intended to cultivate the muscles of paying attention to and accepting what's happening in this moment. Some people create meditation rooms; I meditate wherever I am: the family room sofa, the Adirondack chairs on my front porch, in my car (not while driving, of course), and in my office. I personally feel that cultivating the ability to meditate in an environment that includes people, noise, and movement helps me practice during the busy pace of my ordinary day.

2. **Create a sense of meaning and intent in that space.** No matter where you meditate, take the time to surround yourself with objects that will support your meditation: books, images, a journal, talismans, and other physical reminders of your values (which we'll define for now as the principles by which you want to live your life). I like to keep some of my favorite mindfulness books on my coffee table. The shelves that fill my living room also hold all my cherished books, my Tibetan singing bowl, and pictures of my family, which help me to feel grounded and remind me of my goals and sense of purpose.

   Personally, I'm not a big fan of incense or scented candles; however, if a soft scent enhances your experience, go for it! Just be aware that studies have found synthetic chemicals used in fragrances can interfere with our endocrine systems and serve as hormone disruptors. You may want to do a little research before adding something that can disrupt the natural rhythm of your body. Ultimately, however, the space is all about you, so you should create it in a way that will support you living your best life.

3. **Set the intention to begin.** Before I have entered my meditation space or aligned my posture, I begin by making a commitment to any formal mindfulness practice or meditation. This can be as simple as putting it on my calendar and making time in my day to practice. I also encourage establishing a pre-meditation routine. For me, this routine consists of locking the doors, drinking a glass of water, and using the restroom before adjusting my chair, blankets, or cushions. I also spend a few minutes relaxing my body and getting into the meditation mindset. This may involve reading a poem or a passage from a book (Mary Oliver is one my favorite authors for these moments).

4. **Find your seat.** In meditation, this phrase refers to the act of settling into a comfortable and stable posture for your practice. In finding your seat, you are ensuring your physical position is supported and your body can remain alert, yet relaxed, which can help you achieve a deeper state of mindfulness and inner stillness during the practice. The phrase can also serve as a reminder to let go of any distracting thoughts or physical sensations and to fully focus on the present moment.

    The most recognizable posture for formal meditation is the Lotus posture. This posture is considered the traditional meditation posture and is called *padmasana* in Sanskrit. It involves sitting cross-legged with each foot resting on the opposite thigh. I personally favor what's known as the Burmese posture: this posture involves sitting with both feet pulled in toward the pelvis and the outer side of each foot resting on the ground. I also sit with my torso elevated slightly at the front edge of a cushion.

Know that there are many ways of setting up your body for a formal meditation. Feel free to kneel, resting on your sitting bones (located at the bottom of your pelvis) on a meditation bench or yoga blocks. You may also choose to stand in Mountain Pose. For detailed instruction on alighting your body in this pose, follow the instructions for Mountain Pose included in Chapter 5 Exercises.

You may also sit in a chair with your feet balanced on the floor; in this position, you elongate your spine up to the crown of your head, keep the soft curve at the base of your spine, encourage your shoulders back and down toward your hips, and drop your chin slightly to relax your neck. Some people even lay down with their arms resting comfortably on either side of their body, legs straight, and feet slightly apart.

It's important to remember you will remain in this posture for the duration of the meditation. Set yourself up so you are comfortable. Although physical discomfort can sometimes be a useful focus for meditation, I suggest you align your body in a way that allows you to use your energy to focus on your physical sensations, sounds, breath, or mantra, rather than solely on your body's discomfort. For more detailed instruction on aligning your body for seated meditation, follow the instructions included in the Traditional Body Scan located in the Chapter 3 Exercises.

5. **Consider the posture of your face and hands.** One of my favorite mindfulness teachers is Pema Chödrön,

an ordained Tibetan-Buddhist nun and the author of a series of popular books. She recommends keeping the mouth slightly open so the jaw is relaxed and air can move easily through our noses and mouths. She once joked that this instruction used to result in audiences of people with open, gaping mouths—never her intent. That joke definitely lightened the tone of the room in which she was lecturing, and I smile whenever I remember it. Now, whenever I begin my formal meditation, I spend a moment assessing the level of tension I'm holding in my face and jaw and invite myself to let that tension go.

Chödrön also recommends people practice meditation with their eyes open and a gaze directed comfortably down and in front. I'd always been taught to keep my eyes closed, so I was curious about this suggestion. According to Chödrön, formal mindfulness practice helps prepare us to practice during the course of our days (which most of us spend with our eyes open).

That explanation made a lot of sense to me, so I now meditate with my eyes open. That said, remember your meditation practice is your own. I encourage you to make decisions that feel right to you. The greatest, most compassionate thing you can do for yourself is to mold your formal practice in a way that supports your happiness and well-being.

In the yogic meditation tradition, practitioners sometimes emphasize the movement of their bodies' energy during seated or moving meditation. This can include the act of applying a light pressure to thumbs, fingers, palms of the hands, backs of the hands, curling your fingers, or any other act that moves and directs your body's energy flow in ways that stimulate emotions. Yoga, like Buddhism, includes many symbolic hand gestures and postures known as *mudras*.

Personally, I often return to the traditional hand position called the *jnana mudra*, or the mudra of wisdom. This hand position involves touching the tip of the thumb to the tip of the index finger, while the other fingers remain open and relaxed. For yoginis, this position symbolizes the union of wisdom and knowledge (for me, it's more about signaling my intention to remain open, aware, and comfortable).

A simple Internet or YouTube search will reveal all kinds of mudras that can be used in a meditation practice. If you're curious, practice using these or other hand postures, and pay attention to how you feel physically and emotionally, as well as any thoughts that cross your mind.

Whatever posture you choose in the moment, I suggest you stick with it for the duration of your meditation. As I'll explain in more detail in Chapter 4, I advise adopting only one posture during each meditation session as a way of cultivating stillness and its benefits.

6. **Choose an anchor for your meditation.** In meditation, an "anchor" refers to any technique used to focus and calm the mind. Often, an anchor is a point of reference or an object of attention that helps you stay present and mindful during meditation. This tool provides a focus on which your mind can rest; it also offers a way to center and calm an overactive mind. The anchor, or object of your focus, can be your breath; physical sensations in your body; what you see,

hear, taste, smell, or touch; or a mantra (simple words and phrases repeated in your mind). Your anchor can also be anything else that helps to bring the mind back to the present moment.

Sometimes, an overactive mind can be our best teacher during meditation. Every time your mind wanders, simply notice the thought and compassionately return to your anchor. Resist the temptation to feel discouraged when your mind repeatedly wanders, even during a brief meditation session. I like to think of this process of returning to your anchor as similar to completing a repetition of lifting weights at the gym. Every time you notice you are thinking and then return your attention to your anchor, you've completed a repetition and made your mindfulness "muscle" that much stronger.

7. **Set your alarm or timer.** Even as an experienced meditation teacher, I sometimes have a hard time letting go of thoughts or not worrying about the passage of time while I meditate. Setting a timer is a great way to minimize some of these worries and to avoid the temptation of interrupting your meditation to look at a clock.

Selecting a soothing tone on your smartphone's timer can be a welcome way to end a meditation session. I also enjoy the mobile app *Insight Timer*, which allows you to select the sound, duration of resonance, and number of chimes you'd like to use in a meditation session. In addition to a beginning and ending chime, I usually add middle chimes that remind me to move back into the focus of my meditation or anchor.

8. **Build the habit.** Meditation is like anything else: once it's part of your routine, it's easy to consistently

practice; however, until that time, it's work to create the habit. In my experience, the best way to build the practice is to do it, and to do it the same way each time.

For that reason, you may find it helpful to schedule meditation sessions on whichever calendar app you use and also to set reminders leading up to that time. Schedule your meditation sessions for when you know you will have the space and time, and remember your pre-meditation routine may be as important as your actual meditation practice.

After I've completed my own pre-meditation routine, I set my timer and take the time to align my body. I then take a deep breath in and out, then move my attention to my anchor. With this deliberate process comes energy and commitment, and it gives our brains time to prepare for our practice, even if it's just subconsciously.

Keep in mind that, even with all this preparation and planning, meditation can feel frustrating, and uncomfortable emotions can (and often do) arise. When they do, simply notice them, take a deep breath in and out, re-align your body, and focus your attention on your anchor. And remember: once an action has become a habit, it takes much less thought and energy to perform. Show yourself compassion by creating an easy-to-implement system around your meditation practice.

9. **Send gratitude to yourself and everything that aligned so you could spend time in mediation.** As you conclude your meditation session, take a moment to recognize and appreciate the effort you've made to engage in this practice. Acknowledge the environment

you've created, the time you've set aside, and the intention you brought to your meditation.

Expressing gratitude to yourself and everything that has supported your practice reinforces a positive mindset, encourages consistency, and deepens the connection with your mindfulness journey. Remember, this moment is a reflection of your commitment to personal growth and well-being, and that is something to honor.

You might choose to silently say, "Thank you," or simply smile, acknowledging the peace or insight gained from your meditation. Cultivating this habit of gratitude can enhance the overall experience and benefits of your practice.

Informal Mindfulness Practice

Unlike formal meditation practices, informal mindfulness practices incorporate mindfulness into your daily activities. They can be practiced anytime and anywhere, so long as you are able to be fully present in the moment and pay attention to your thoughts, feelings, and physical sensations without judgment. Informal practices are a great way to bring mindfulness to your everyday life and reduce stress and anxiety while improving your overall well-being.

The 5, 4, 3, 2, 1 Informal Meditation (2 Minutes)

This practice comes from the Teachers Personal Development course, *Introduction to Mindfulness: A Practical Guide to Living Mindfully for Educators*. It was created by my team at Mind Body Align and is intended to establish stability by leading you through your five senses. This exercise can be used anytime you notice yourself feeling anxious or disconnected. This informal meditation also brings your awareness to the present moment by focusing your attention on something tangible in your environment.

To begin, find a comfortable seated position that reflects your intention to be alert yet relaxed in the practice.

5 - Look around your environment and silently name **five** things you see.

4 - If it is comfortable, close your eyes, and, in your head, name **four** things you hear.

3 - And when you're ready, name **three** things you can feel on your skin or within the structure of your body.

2 - Breathing in, note **two** things you can smell.

1 - Open your mouth and breathe in air across your taste buds, and silently name **one** thing you can taste.

Now, gently move your awareness back to your breath if that is comfortable for you. Then open your eyes if you have them closed. Notice how you feel, and the sensations in your body. Take in your environment with fresh senses, more deeply connected to the environment you are in, and know you can return to this practice anytime.

Take a moment to send gratitude to yourself and all the things that align in order for you to be present in this moment.

••• 2 •••

The Benefits of a Mindfulness Practice

A WHILE BACK, my husband and nephew spent six months training for a Tough Mudder, those popular obstacle races that require contestants to climb over walls, slither through mud, and leap over fire. Every week, they each worked through a training regimen that included gym workouts, early morning runs, and preparation for the obstacle courses.

Some obstacles challenged physical fitness, such as climbing over tall walls, running up 20-foot ramps, swinging from a rope over a big water pit, and catching monkey bars in mid-air. Others challenged their pain threshold by requiring them to swim in an ice bath or run through electric wires.

Participants weren't told about the specific obstacles in their event until a week before the race, so that also meant my husband and nephew had to be prepared for anything. They spent hours in the gym, running outside, and mentally preparing for whatever might come their way.

The race itself was just as grueling as my husband and nephew had anticipated, but they finished with an incredible sense of accomplishment—and a newfound appreciation for their own potential. In fact, the experience was so rewarding they went on to finish several other Tough Mudders competitions as well, each time discovering their preparation and inherent bravery was more than up to the challenge.

Similarly, we practice mindfulness for the Tough Mudder that is life. There's a wonderful phrase in Sanskrit that loosely translates as, "We practice yoga to undo the suffering yet to come."

The same can be said about mindfulness meditation: by practicing on ordinary or even great days, we prepare ourselves for the inevitable challenges that are a part of being human. In this chapter, we'll explore the science behind this practice and why it's so beneficial, particularly when it comes to minimizing suffering and maximizing happiness. We'll not only explore how the brain works, but why this big, bossy organ so often tricks us into negative or unhelpful thoughts. Most importantly, I'll illustrate how mindfulness allows us to restructure this wiring in order to live happier, more fulfilled lives.

Getting out of the Funhouse: Squaring our Perceptions and Reality

No doubt you've heard (and probably even used) the expression, "Seeing is believing." These days, most people use it as a way of explaining how we verify that things are true—especially things that seem unlikely.

For instance, you might think I'm delusional if I told you I witnessed a raccoon who could juggle. However, if I brought you my little masked friend and encouraged him to demonstrate his remarkable ability to keep three golf balls aloft, you'd undoubtedly be a lot more inclined to take me at my word.

Many of us also use variations of "seeing is believing" to acknowledge when extraordinary incidents have come to pass, whether that's a teenager who finally cleans their room unprompted, a habitually tardy friend who beats us to a lunch date, or when the person who swore they couldn't (and wouldn't) bake proudly presents a gorgeous souffle for dinner.

The phrase was coined by Thomas Fuller, a 17th century English clergyman. And it's actually only the first half of Fuller's famous aphorism. The cleric's full assertion was actually, "Seeing is believing, but feeling is truth."

And that, in a nutshell, is the beauty of mindfulness.

A mindfulness practice allows us to experience our sensations more clearly and fully. It encourages us to be fully present to the sound of a string quartet, the feel of a kitten's fur, or the taste of the summer's first strawberries. By removing the distractions of thoughts, worries, or judgments, we can be more present to these experiences and the gifts they have to offer.

As a way of proving this for yourself, think about the last snack you ate in front of the TV or in a movie theater. Maybe it was popcorn with extra butter, a bag of M&Ms, or your favorite cookie. Try to remember the experience of eating that snack: the texture, the way it engaged your tastebuds, the emotions evoked while you munched.

If you're like most people, you might not have noticed some of these details while in front of the screen—and especially if the movie or show was especially compelling. As a contrast to this divided experience, sit down at a table with no other distractions (if you really want to amplify the experience, consider also wearing a blindfold).

Now, try a few bites of the snack and really focus on the experience. Does your sensory engagement change? My guess is it becomes a lot more vivid—and you'll enjoy the snack a lot more. Why? Because you are eating it with mindful intent and focusing your thoughts on that sensory experience, rather than masking or dividing them with competing stimuli.

But that's only half of it. Just like Fuller's full aphorism, mindfulness also encourages us to tap into our feelings—and what we believe to be true. To understand how, let's go back to this idea of seeing (or tasting, or any of the other senses, for that matter).

As vivid as our senses can be, the data they provide is really only useful once our brain has processed it. Why? Simply put, it's because our five physical senses are really just neurons that respond to a particular kind of stimuli (for instance, our eyes contain receptors that respond to change in light or color; our taste buds register bitter, sweet, and other categories of flavor). These sensory receptors then telegraph stimuli to the brain, which processes and organizes the information sent by the cells, thereby turning a sensation into a perception.

And it is through all that processing and organizing that we are able to make meaning out of the physical experience.

Say you were raised on a deserted island, where your only visual experience was the sand, palm trees, ocean, and changing sky. You've seen the full spectrum of color, but the meaning you've assigned to them is probably quite limited (for instance, the color red might signal a beautiful sunset and the promise of gorgeous weather the next day; the color green might indicate a coconut is too young to eat or a snake is poisonous).

Now, imagine you are whisked off that island and dropped at a busy intersection. You look up at the traffic light and see the color green. Based on your previous perceptions, you might assume that's a signal to stop. Similarly, you may interpret red as a signal to go.

Why? Because your previous interpretations of these colors have led you to make these conclusions.

Our accumulating perceptions are also what cause us to begin assigning value to certain sensory stimuli, why some of us might prefer the sound of a string quartet, while others of us might rather listen to angry death metal. In time, those perceptions also begin to dictate what we do (and do not) sense. Consider this famous optical illusion, first titled "My Wife/My Mother-in-Law":

When you first look at this image, do you see a young woman dressed to go out for the evening, or an old woman wearing a kerchief and shawl?

Ever since this image was first published in 1915, generations have delighted in the game of which woman they first see and how to find her counterpart as well. However, it was only recently that cognitive scientists began to understand why some of us see the younger woman and others see her elder.

A 2021 study published in the scholarly journal *Nature* found respondents tended to first identify the woman who most closely approximated them in age; in other words, younger people were more likely to first spy the wife, while older participants saw the mother-in-law. The reason is subconscious bias—in this case, our tendency to identify more with our peers rather than those individuals who come from other generations, a phenomenon psychologists call "age anchoring."[1]

In other words, it's not so much that optical illusions like this one play tricks on our senses as it is our minds themselves doing the tomfoolery. Whether it's because of distractions, habits, beliefs, prejudices, or other pre-existing ideas, we all often struggle to make an objective assessment of sensory stimuli.

Instead, we give our brains free reign to make judgments based on previous perceptions, and we rarely stop to question the impact of those mental machinations. Consequently, we become less and less in touch with our sensations and the realities they depict in favor of a distorted version of reality based on preconceptions and biases.

To understand why, consider our species' collective time on this planet. Our minds have evolved to seek out patterns and to use these patterns as tools to keep us free from harm. Whether we are conscious of it or not, our brains are constantly making judgments about what will keep us safe, whether that means we sniff a carton of milk to see if the contents have soured or we habitually look both ways before crossing the street, even if there's a *One Way* sign right in front of us. These survival skills kept us alive for millennia, and so many of us never stop to interrogate them.

But they don't always serve us in the present day.

That's at least in part because another way our brains operate to keep us safe is by emphasizing potentially harmful and challenging events over favorable and successful events. That tendency, coupled with our capacity for making quick judgments, means our perspective of the world isn't always accurate, nor is our sense of proportion. Left to its own devices, the mind loves to exploit the potential for harm and to encourage us to be protective when we don't always need to be.

As a result, reality can begin to look like a kind of carnival funhouse mirror, where past hurts become exaggerated and make us distrust present affection, and where biases and fears prevent us from embracing opportunities for new connections or novel experiences. Mindfulness allows us to identify those filters and the narratives we associate with them.

Just as importantly, it empowers us to walk past the funhouse mirror versions of reality in favor of a more accurate depiction of the world as it truly is.

By making us more conscious of our sensory stimuli and the meaning we assign to it, we also learn more about the world as it is and our relationship to it. As the great mindfulness teacher and Zen master Thich Nhat Hanh once wrote:

> Mindfulness is the miracle by which we master and restore ourselves. Consider, for example: a magician who cuts his body into many parts and places each part in a different region—hands in the south, arms in the east, legs in the north, and then by some miraculous power lets forth a cry that reassembles whole every part of his body. Mindfulness

is like that—it is the miracle that can call back in a flash our dispersed mind and restore it to wholeness so that we can live each minute of life.[2]

If you're like me, it's a lot easier to believe these and other assertions if they are also backed up by science. Happily, the last decade or so has given rise to hundreds of scholarly studies and articles about the benefits of mindfulness. And thanks to these skilled researchers, we know that mindfulness—and meditation in particular—literally builds the parts of our brain responsible for paying attention and for processing sensory information, just like lifting weights builds our biceps and triceps.[3]

Studies have also found that mindfulness not only improves our ability to focus but also our working memories. [4] Mindfulness also helps train our brains to discard distractions that might skew our perceptions, which allows us to embrace our sensations and thoughts with greater clarity and confidence.[5] In other words, mindfulness provides the tools to trust what we see, feel, and believe. And that, in turn, allows us to more fully embrace the gifts offered to us simply by being human.

Hardwiring for Happiness

When I first began practicing mindfulness, I was inspired in part by people like the Dalai Lama and Desmond Tutu. In addition to being strong, impactful leaders, they both had an admirable calm and peacefulness about them—a wisdom about the world that seemed to emanate from the core of their being. I wanted to emulate that quiet strength in what I did as well, and I had the intuition that mindful awareness practices would help me get there.

Turns out, I was on to something.

In 2003, a team of researchers at the University of Rochester set out to prove an empirical connection between mindfulness and a person's psychological well-being (a very scholarly way to say their *happiness*). These scholars amassed a group of more than 300 study participants and asked them to complete a survey that gauged the degree to which the individuals practiced a mindful life. To tease that out, the researchers asked respondents how strongly they agreed with statements such as:

1. I'm not always conscious of my emotions until some time later.

2. I tend to break or spill things because I'm distracted or not paying attention.

3. I find it difficult to stay focused on the present moment.

4. I tend to "multi-task" throughout the day.

5. I snack without being wholly aware of what—or how much—I am eating.

The psychologists then administered a series of surveys and tests to determine the participants' level of self-awareness, self-confidence, and self-satisfaction. What they found was a direct correlation between an individual's mindfulness and their overall psychological well-being.

As the researchers explain in their article, "The Benefits of Being Present: Mindfulness and Its Role in Psychological Well-Being," there are several reasons why.[6] First, the surveys revealed that participants with higher mindfulness scores were better equipped to experience pleasurable sensations and emotions.

Because these individuals were able to focus their attention on enjoyable experiences, such as watching a beautiful sunrise, eating a particularly delicious piece of chocolate, or dancing to a favorite song, they also reported higher levels of pleasure and joy in those experiences than people who were less mindful.

The mindful individuals were also able to bank their intense feelings of happiness, which ultimately had the effect of allowing these positive experiences to last longer—and remain more vivid—in their minds. That, in turn, contributed to their overall happiness and sense of vitality.

The researchers also discovered that individuals who scored higher on the mindfulness survey were more in tune with their emotional states. Not only did that awareness allow them to better identify and fulfill their needs for comfort, solace, solitude, or other helpful coping mechanisms, it also meant that these participants were better able to shift from a negative to a more positive emotional experience.[7]

That's in large part because these individuals also had the ability to disengage from unhelpful or even destructive habits and beliefs. We'll talk more about this phenomenon in Chapter 5; for now, it's enough to know the practice of mindfulness makes it easier to choose behaviors and dispositions that serve us. Consequently, people who practice mindfulness have been found to have lower rates of stress, anxiety, and depression. They also report experiencing greater optimism, empathy, autonomy, and existential satisfaction.[8]

Let's take a look at how all of this works in practice. Say an argument brews between you and a loved one. Without a regular mindfulness practice, you'll most likely find yourself reacting with the same habituated responses you've developed throughout your life, whether that's avoidance, passive aggressive behavior, or self-righteous shouting. The more we practice mindfulness, the easier it becomes to recognize those impulses and to chart a healthier course.

With the help of a mindfulness practice, we can notice when we become triggered. Instead of immediately acting on that emotional experience, we can then name it and make a conscious choice about whether to respond and how. By simply acknowledging an emotion (quietly saying, something like *I'm feeling resentful, I'm feeling hurt,* or *I'm feeling impatient*), we take away a lot of the power that emotion has over us.

Naming it also gives us the cognitive distance to redirect, whether that's articulating our emotion to our loved one (*Honey, I'm beginning to feel really anxious*), asking for what we need (*Hey, I think it's better if I take a break from this conversation until I'm feeling more grounded*) or—ideally—both (*Sweetheart, I'm feeling really frustrated right now. Let's pause and try talking again tomorrow*).

In these moments, mindfulness allows us to remove our armor and be honest and vulnerable—both with ourselves and with our loved ones. That vulnerability and honesty, in turn, can radically transform our relationships for the better—and dramatically increase our personal happiness along the way.

By simply being present to our thoughts and sensations with awareness and acceptance, we can begin to experience the world both in real-time and as it truly is. We become better at making conscious choices regarding our behavior. And each time we do, we take a step toward becoming our very best selves.

For instance, if you're the kind of person who is prone to screaming like a banshee when you're triggered, you may find a mindfulness practice affords you the ability to just walk away from unnecessary conflict. If you're someone who will do anything to avoid confrontation, you may find you now have the courage to speak up and address a problem or injustice. In these moments of self-actualization, you'll also find what once felt like a scheduled practice has now become a powerful way of life.

Building a Better Brain (and Body)

Beginning around 2010, patients at New York University's prestigious Langone Medical Center began noticing an unusual phenomenon: the waiting room of the hospital's radiology department was increasingly populated by Buddhist monks, most of whom arrived in their traditional bright orange and burgundy monastic robes.

As it turned out, these professional meditators weren't at all sick; they were part of a pioneering study to chart the impact of meditation on the brain. Day after day, these monks agreed to be loaded into a massive magnetic resonance imaging (MRI) scanner. Once situated, they were asked to meditate while neuroscientists on the other side of the glass took images of the monks' brains.

What the researchers discovered in these scans was nothing short of astounding.[9] For starters, the more the monks meditated, the larger their brains grew. Specifically, their gray matter—the prefrontal cortex and hippocampus, which are involved in attention, memory, and emotional regulation—increased in as little as eight weeks.

That growth is significant: our brains need optimal surface area in order for neurons to function, which is why they have all those hills, grooves, and canyons instead of a flat surface. The larger a brain's surface area, the better its neurological functions. When it comes to the prefrontal cortex and hippocampus, additional gray matter improves our attention, memory, and emotional regulation.

Not only does this additional surface area make for greater happiness, it also helps to prevent conditions like Alzheimer's Disease and dementia. Because we all naturally lose gray matter over time anyway, anything we can do to increase its strength and volume also increases our brain's ability to function properly in later years. The subsequent research from this study indicates that regular meditation practice may help slow this process and even promote the growth of new brain cells.

And here's the best news of all: the more you struggle to stay focused during meditation, the more gray matter you will build. Why? The NYU researchers speculate it's because of how the brain is organized. Our minds operate simultaneously on two separate networks: the extrinsic network, which is dedicated to external tasks, such as brushing our teeth or having a conversation with a loved one; and the intrinsic network, which is responsible for our thoughts and emotions.

The default factory setting for our brains is such that we tend to use only one of these networks at a time. However, the monks' MRIs demonstrated that each time they pulled their attention from the extrinsic back to the intrinsic, they were also building a stronger connection between the two. The more they practiced this switch, the more they were able to utilize both operating systems simultaneously.

The NYU researchers also discovered that meditation strengthens connections between the left and right hemispheres of the brain. As a result, we now know mindfulness can also enhance cognitive flexibility, creativity, and a more balanced state of mind.

And that's just the start. Mindfulness has been proven to impact our bodies as well, improving our immune systems, our ability to fight chronic disease, and our capacity for pain management. The real leader in this field of mindfulness is Jon Kabat-Zinn, who pioneered the concept of mindfulness-based stress reduction to aid individuals suffering from chronic pain.

Instead of prescribing medication to dull the pain, Kabat-Zinn taught these patients how to experience their pain in a more manageable way; namely, by making friends with it through mindful meditation. Doing so dramatically reduced their suffering and allowed these individuals to live with greater happiness and fewer limitations.

What all of the aforementioned studies have in common is scientific proof that even a casual mindfulness practice offers tremendous benefits for our bodies, minds, and souls. As little as fifteen minutes a day will result in real, tangible improvements in just a matter of weeks.

In the remaining chapters of this book, we'll delve into more of the hows and the whys. I'll also provide additional tips and tools that will allow you to enjoy these benefits more fully. For now, all you really need to do is commit to a mindfulness practice.

Of course, sometimes that's easier said than done. So many of us (myself included) often forget to practice mindfulness and meditation at the times we need it most. In response to that reality, I always like to return to a little saying often attributed to Gandhi. It goes something like, "Everyone should meditate at least a half an hour a day—unless you're too busy, in which case, you should meditate for an hour." I don't know if Gandhi ever actually said that, but I love the idea.

It's almost always true that the times we think we're too busy to stop and be mindful are when we most need to practice. Knowing that, consider ways you can ensure that mindfulness remains a part of your day, no matter how overwhelming it might feel.

For instance, just as a wedding ring reminds us of our commitment to our spouse and marriage, it can be helpful to have a tangible reminder to be mindful. When my life feels particularly hectic, I often put on a wristband or bracelet that reminds me of my commitment to mindfulness practice and the importance of taking the time simply to notice. Other times, I'll set an alarm on my phone as a signal I need to stop and be present for a few breaths. That pause is often all it takes for my body and mind to relax.

As an experiment, the next time you feel triggered, commit to pausing long enough to observe the sensation of your feet on the floor. If you're wearing shoes, how do they or your socks feel around your feet? If you're barefoot or in flip-flops, what is the sensation of the air on your toes? Do they feel warm? Cold? That simple observation can calm the brain and mind, taking us from a state of stress to one of ease. By regularly engaging in simple exercises such as this one, you'll most likely find greater acceptance and love for both yourself and others.

In general, both of these outcomes are beneficial. However, it's also important to note here that there are times when being vulnerable with others does not serve us.

As an empath, I know I am particularly susceptible to toxic energies and situations. I've learned over time there are some people I need to approach from within a safe and nurturing bubble, where they don't have the power to hurt me. Other empaths have told me they like to use the image of a suit of armor or a protective wall. Personally, I particularly like the bubble imagery since it still protects me, but it doesn't require me to hide behind stiff, heavy metal or an imposing rock edifice.

I am free to move about the world unimpeded, knowing my beautiful, gossamer bubble will protect me. If you are in a relationship with a narcissist or otherwise toxic human, having a bubble or similar image can be a useful technique for remaining true to your mindfulness work without opening yourself up to the potential for real harm.

Mindfulness also allows us to make informed decisions about when it's advantageous to be wholly vulnerable and when we're better off hopping into our bubbles (or suit of armor or whatever imagery is most effective for you). Either way, you can feel confident in knowing you made an honest, informed choice about what was best for you in that situation. And because mindfulness also always encourages us to pause and reflect, you'll have myriad opportunities to revise or change your decision along the way!

Chapter 2 Takeaways

- Mindfulness helps remove distracting thoughts and judgments, which allows us to experience our sensations more fully.

- The human brain is hardwired to find patterns and to identify danger, which means we're programmed to look for both, even when it's not necessarily warranted.

- Sensations become perceptions after our brain processes the sensory data and assigns meaning to it. This processing helps us to understand and categorize the physical experience, but it can also cause us to skew or assign unhelpful meanings to it.

- The more we allow our brains to make judgments based on biases, habits, and beliefs, the less in touch we are with our sensations and the realities they depict.

- Mindfulness improves both our ability to focus and to discard distractions and prejudices that can taint or skew our perceptions.

- Practitioners of mindfulness tend to be more in touch with their emotions, especially those that are pleasurable or joyful, which also leads to increased happiness and vitality.

- Mindfulness practitioners are also better equipped to identify negative emotions and ascertain what they need in such moments. This, in turn, allows them to proactively identify what they need in those situations rather than simply reacting out of habit or impulse.

- Studies have shown a mindfulness practice increases the brain's gray matter, which is responsible for attention, memory, and emotional regulation. An increase in gray matter has also been correlated with a decreased chance of Alzheimer's Disease and dementia.

- Other benefits of mindfulness include greater cognitive flexibility and creativity, as well as an enhanced ability to manage and respond to pain.

Chapter 2 Exercises

Formal Mindfulness Practice

Circle Breathing

This exercise can go with you everywhere and is a steady friend when wanting a moment to increase wise thinking. When you're ready, quietly inhale for a count of four, then exhale for that same count of four. Focus your attention on the breath as it enters and exits your body. Inhale: 1-2-3-4, Exhale: 1-2-3-4.

If you are able, expand this exercise by gently pausing your breath between the inhale and exhale. Inhale: 1-2-3-4, Pause your breath: 1-2-3-4, Exhale: 1-2-3-4, Pause: 1-2-3-4. When you notice your mind has wandered (as our minds are naturally inclined to do), kindly move your attention back to the felt sensations of your body breathing; focus on the rhythm of your inhale and your exhale.

Continue for a few full cycles or as long as you like. You may also choose this meditation as an anchor for your formal meditation practice by "finding your seat" and setting a timer (ten minutes is gold!).

Alternate Nostril Breathing

You can turn the circle breath meditation into alternate nostril breathing by first closing one nostril and then the other. Gently press your left and then your right nostril, shutting the nostrils alternately with a thumb or index finger. You may also choose to simply imagine inhaling and exhaling through alternate nostrils. Inhale through the left, closing the right, switch, then exhale from the right while closing the left.

You may choose to count the rhythm quietly while saying the instructions along with the count. Inhale (left) -3-4, Pause -2-3-4. Exhale (right) -3-4, Pause 2-3-4. Inhale (left) -3-4, pause -2-3-4, exhale (right) -3-4, pause 2-3-4. When you're ready, return your breath to its normal rhythm, knowing you can return to this breathing exercise any time and place you wish.

Informal Mindfulness Practice

I'm Brushing My Teeth

This is an exercise that encourages you to begin and end each day with a short mindfulness practice. There's nothing to add to your calendar here. The practice is to simply notice what's happening during an ordinary activity you perform habitually and to turn that mindless habit into a *mindful* moment.

While brushing your teeth, for example, bring your attention to the hand holding your toothbrush. Notice the felt sensations: the pressure of the handle, the vibration of the movement, the shifting position of your thumb as you move the brush along your upper and lower teeth or from right to left (or left to right).

When you're ready, shift your attention to the opposite hand. Where is it located? If it's resting on your bathroom counter or vanity top, notice the temperature and texture on that surface. If it's on your hip or cheek, observe the feel of your skin or clothes.

When you're ready, move your attention to the conversation in your head. Hear your thoughts as if you are listening to a morning or evening radio show, with a degree of separation between you and your musings. Simply listen as you would to the reflections of someone you love.

Finally, take a deep breath in and out, and set an intention for your day or your night.

... 3 ...
The Mind-Body Connection

ANYONE WHO KNOWS me also knows I am a dog lover.

Several years ago, my husband and I had two gorgeous German shepherds. Both were black and tan, but their personalities were utterly distinct. Sophie, the older, was as particular and headstrong as she was beautiful. Even as a puppy, she had strong opinions. If you picked her up, she wanted to be back on the ground. Once on the ground, she wanted to be picked up again. One dog bed was too soft, another too hard. She was always just so persnickety. But that didn't stop me and my husband from adoring her.

My sister-in-law gave us Sophie as a gift not long after we were married. She's a veterinarian in Colorado and had done a favor for a well-known breeder there. To say thank you, the breeder offered my sister-in-law the pick of the litter, and she picked Sophie. It didn't take long for me to realize just how smart that little puppy was, so I named her after the Latin word for *wisdom*.

My husband took the liberty of naming our second dog, *Aprilia*, after the Italian motorcycle. Like her namesake, Aprilia was sleek and sporty, with shorter hair than her very fluffy adoptive sister and a streamlined body, no matter how much we fed her.

We adopted Aprilia from our local shelter, where the workers said they could tell she'd already had a rough life. Sophie was not impressed by her sudden appearance. The two dogs would fight—awful, violent battles that would some-times draw blood. Initially, my husband and I would break it up, but my veterinarian sister-in-law eventually counseled us to let the two dogs have it out; they needed to find their place with one another, and we couldn't help with that.

She was right. After multiple visits to our local veterinar-ian to stitch up the wounded, the two shepherds reached a kind of truce with one another. They were never best friends, so far as we humans could tell, but they tolerated each other well enough.

Around us, Aprilia was a total lover. It was almost as if she knew she'd been saved and was beside herself with gratitude she constantly needed to express. She was affectionate with both me and my husband and was also deeply protective of me. Whenever someone would come over to visit, she'd sit on my feet as if guarding me.

Sophie, on the other hand, was always a little more aloof. She'd often sit on the other side of the room, surveying what was happening both inside and outside.

Our farmhouse has always been a great place to be a dog. We installed a huge invisible fence that gave the dogs ten acres of land they could roam. They'd spend hours hunting rabbits or just sniffing in the grass. Behind the house, the land is wooded and slopes down to a lovely little pond. Next to it is a field we've let grow wild, and beyond that are our neighbor's corn and soybean fields. Geese often congregate in the fields and around the pond, and the dogs loved chasing those big, squawking birds.

One day, seemingly out of the blue, Aprilia developed a fatal digestive problem. My husband and I were devastated. As it turns out, so was Sophie. By then, she was an old dog— about twelve years old, which is elderly for shepherds. She'd had arthritis for a while, but she still loved going for walks.

After Aprilia died, Sophie lost interest. We'd coax her to go outside and walk down the lane with us, but she always wanted to turn around and go home. During the day, she'd just mope around, mostly lying on the garage floor and barely moving.

One day, not long after Aprilia died, I came home to find that Sophie had finally left the garage. Initially, I was glad; it was a cool spring afternoon, and the sun had left tiny pockets of snow on the ground—a perfect day to be a dog with a big, active nose. I thought maybe Sophie had found a way through her grief and was back out exploring.

I called her name and began searching our yard but couldn't find her. I began to worry that maybe she'd run away (an old trick from her much younger years). I called my husband, who jumped into his car, to come home and help me look.

Eventually, I made my way to the back of the house, where a series of steep steps led down to the pond. About halfway down, there's a right angle in the steps that is lined with large rocks covered in moss. I found Sophie there, lying motionless and looking out at the water.

By then, she'd grown hypothermic, and her eyes looked as if they'd been covered in cataracts. We took her to the vet, who told us her chances of survival were slim. We made the heart-wrenching decision to put her down. Unlike Aprilia's death, Sophie's was peaceful. We could at least give her that.

The grief that followed was shattering. My dogs have always been like my children, and I'd lost two of them in just a few months. I felt that loss immensely. One day that summer, I spied a flock of geese in the field as I was walking down to the pond. I thought about how both dogs—and Sophie in particular—used to love chasing them.

I remembered the way Sophie would crouch in that characteristic shepherd pose before flying down the hill in hot pursuit, her ears and tongue flapping as fast as she ran. The geese would erupt in a cacophonous cloud, and she would pause, a huge smile on her face, so delighted she'd caused all that ruckus. It was one of the closest things I'd ever seen to unbridled joy.

That afternoon, as I walked to the pond, I recalled Sophie's joy. I felt the warm sun on my skin and took in how green and lush the landscape looked. In that moment, it was as if the spirit of Sophie had taken over. Before I even fully knew what I was doing, I began racing toward the geese, flapping my arms like a banshee. The geese took off, honking and squawking, and I knew Sophie would have been pleased.

More than that, it was as if she were running alongside me with that big, goofy dog smile on her face. I still missed her terribly and mourned her death, but that grief was now marked with gratitude as well—gratefulness for all the dogs had shared and taught me. In that moment, I experienced my own joy.

I've yet to meet anyone who enjoys feeling the kind of grief I experienced when I lost Sophie and Aprilia, nor anyone who willingly seeks out that kind of sadness. Certainly, I don't. But what I've learned from my years of mindfulness study is they are an inevitable part of being human. Feelings come in a package: we don't get to pick and choose which ones to keep and which ones to discard. And whether we like it or not, feelings like grief and joy are bound together, sometimes seeming like two sides of the same coin.

Too many of us try to turn off unpleasant feelings like grief or sadness, hoping to avoid the pain that comes with them. But when we do, we become disconnected from our bodies and our lived experiences. We also lose our capacity for happiness and joy, the other side of those emotional spheres.

In my experience, the grief we feel when we lose someone (human or fur-baby) is directly related to the love and depth of feeling we have for them. The more joyful experiences we have with someone, the more sadness we're bound to find without those experiences. Cutting off that sadness means cutting off our ability to remember joy and love as well.

Mindfulness allows us to make room for all of those feelings, even when they seem unpleasant or scary. It teaches us to embrace our whole selves, not just the beautiful parts or the ones we're most proud of. The consistent act of practicing mindfulness develops the skills needed to recognize and learn how to accept all aspects of being human, no matter what feelings or experiences come our way.

I have a favorite quote by the great Zen monk Shunryu Suzuki that gets at this very idea: *You are perfect as you are, and there is always room for improvement.* It's kind of like a *koan*; those paradoxical statements or riddles in Buddhism are intended to spark insight and even enlightenment.

In this case, I really like the conundrum that it's possible to be simultaneously perfect and continually evolving. And while I still haven't found the answer to that riddle, merely contemplating it is a powerful reminder that we are special, unique, and always growing.

Holding that idea in our hearts and minds can dramatically change how we live our lives. It gives us the grace to remain on our mindfulness journeys; it also provides insight into the people around us and helps us build compassion and empathy.

Emotions are also like Suzuki's koan. While it may seem paradoxical, we often experience two very contrasting emotions in a single moment. Recognizing this truth helps achieve a place where we can be curious about the variety of thoughts and sensations happening in our mind and body and even choose between those emotions.

That doesn't mean we suppress or ignore some of these feelings. We can choose to focus our awareness on one of multiple emotions that may be present. That's what happened to me that afternoon with the geese. I was simultaneously grief-stricken and joyful. And as I raced toward the flock of birds, I chose joy—and I embraced it with my whole heart.

Choosing joy—choosing any emotion, really—begins first with choosing to connect with our bodies. In this chapter, we'll explore both the neuroscience behind the brain-body connection as well as the benefits that come to those who embrace that connection as part of their mindfulness journey.

Along the way, we'll explore how an awareness of this connection allows us to become more intentional about embracing and processing our feelings as they arise.

Brains, Hearts, Guts, Oh My!

One of the things I admire most about dogs is just how fully they live in their own bodies. Most of the canines I've encountered delight wholeheartedly in the act of running through a field or wrestling with one another.

When I raced after that flock of geese, part of my joy came from my own physical sensation of racing down that hill. I wasn't worried about what anyone else would think or whether I looked foolish or what was on my schedule for later in the day. Instead, I was fully present to the feelings of my feet, legs, hips, and arms as they navigated the uneven hillside and propelled me toward the startled geese. I felt the shape of my smile and the wind blowing my hair out behind me. My whole body heard the geese's aversion to my approach and the subsequent vibration of their wings moving the air.

As adults, we tend to forget what it is to have wholly embodied experiences. Speaking personally, I know I often decide I'm too busy (or old) for such shenanigans. However, that also means I miss out on the gifts those moments have to offer.

As the talented psychologist and mindfulness teacher Tara Brach notes, it's no coincidence that the Chinese word for "busy" translates literally as *heart-death*: the busier we get, the more time we spend planning and thinking about what we have to do next, and the less energy we have for the present moment.

That also means we lose sight of how we actually feel. We become disconnected from our hearts and fail to recognize what that all-important organ is telling us. The same is true for our bellies. No matter how many times we talk about our "gut instincts," most of us ignore those messages in favor of whatever story our brains are creating. We miss out on wisdom that is hard-wired into our bodies, and we ignore or don't understand important signs and signals that help us navigate the world.

Scientists are now learning just how interconnected our brains, hearts, and guts really are. Neurologists, for instance, have discovered that the heart contains tens of thousands of neurons that form their own little nervous system and communicate directly with the brain.[1] Our stomachs and intestines, meanwhile, not only produce hormones that communicate with the brain, they are also responsible for churning out key neurochemicals, including serotonin, which regulates cognitive processes and moods.

Not only that, but groundbreaking studies by Duke University researchers have found synapses in our gut cells as well.[2] In that regard, we actually have three brains: one in our skull, one in our chest, and one in our gut. Researchers say that's just the beginning of our true brain-body connection. The cells in other organs and tissues also help contribute to what we think of as our mind or "self." In other words, what we've long thought of as "intuition" or a visceral feeling is actually important knowledge emanating from deep within.

As a middle-aged woman, I've certainly experienced the truth of that connection firsthand. Ask anyone experiencing perimenopause just how out-of-control hormones can make us feel (for that matter, you can probably ask her partner or kids as well). For my own part, I spent way too long trying to manage hot flashes and mood swings on my own before finally seeking out the help of a functional medicine doctor (a holistically-focused doctor who considers the interconnectedness of the body's systems to identify and treat the root causes of disease).

At my first appointment, I explained how volatile my emotions had become and how much difficulty I was having regulating them on my own. She ran tests and discovered I actually had a mild version of leaky gut syndrome, a condition in which the lining of the small intestine becomes damaged, causing undigested food particles, toxins, and bacteria to leak into the bloodstream, potentially triggering inflammation and a range of health issues.

She also explained the digestive systems and brains are closely connected, and what happens in the gut can affect our emotional state and the thoughts we think. This connection is known as the gut-brain axis, and it works through a complex network of nerves, hormones, and other signaling molecules that travel between the gut and the brain.[3]

When the digestive system is working properly, it helps regulate our emotions and thoughts, but when it is disrupted, it can have a negative impact on our mental health. The gut contains billions of bacteria, collectively known as the gut microbiome, which also play an important role in our mental health and well-being.

A healthy gut microbiome can help regulate our mood, reduce anxiety, and improve cognitive function. On the other hand, an imbalance in the gut microbiome can lead to mental health problems and even cognitive decline.[4] Once, I was on a whole-food diet and taking a powerful probiotic; I was blown away by how quickly my moods improved.

Science has shown that eating nourishing foods, intentionally moving our bodies, and managing fluctuating hormone levels may all contribute to our overall mental health. Similarly, mindfulness can help us pay attention to what information different parts of our bodies, like our guts, have to report.

It also encourages us to listen to the wisdom these organs and systems have to offer. Allowing those brains, our whole body, and our mind to inform our next actions, no matter how large or small, is a surefire way to ensure we are making holistic, intentional decisions for ourselves.

Knowing that, I'm always surprised by just how many of my new clients arrive disconnected from their physical bodies and the sensations that happen there. As we begin our mindfulness work, I ask questions that invite these clients to begin just hanging out with the felt sensation of their in-the-moment experiences, rather than mentally constructing a narrative about those experiences.

One way I do this is to ask these clients how certain situations or moments feel in their bodies. Where, specifically, do they notice physical sensations? What do they notice about the sensation: Does it have a texture, color, smell, or taste?

Often, new clients will respond with, *I don't know. I don't feel it anywhere. I don't notice anything.* And then, they jump back into recounting a memory from their past, expressing a fear for their future, or reporting a judgment about their experience in the present moment. This storytelling inevitably disconnects them from what's happening here and now.

I understand the difficulty. Quieting the conversations in our head by repeatedly returning our focused attention to the felt experiences of our body can feel impractical and maybe even impossible.

However, we have so much to gain by taking time to listen to what our bodies are saying. Sometimes, the easiest way to do that is to move the focus of your attention to a particular point on your body. A simple way to do so is to begin by asking yourself the question, *Where do I notice physical sensations?* You can also conduct a body scan, a formal mindfulness exercise I detail at the end of this chapter.

Many new mindfulness practitioners tell me they initially find it difficult to focus on their body with deep awareness, especially when they're in the midst of chaos or high-stress situations.

I can empathize.

There are still plenty of times when I lose track of the insight this practice can provide. Here's an example from just this morning when I awoke agitated about a long drive to a meeting I didn't really want to attend. I was also distracted about an upcoming trip my husband and I had planned and how much work needed to be done in preparation for it, including packing clothes and moving them to our camper.

The combination of both preoccupations meant I wasn't being mindful of—well, *anything*. I left the house without the suitcase I'd intended to leave in the camper, and I showed up at the meeting practically vibrating with frustration and anxiety. I sat down, clenching and unclenching my jaw. My shoulders and neck were like granite, and I could feel a knot of pressure growing along the top of my eyebrows.

Because I was distracted and agitated, I'd ignored those physical sensations earlier in the morning. I'd also overlooked a series of mind-numbing hot flashes, an insatiable thirst, and the fact that my mood was somehow managing to flush itself even further down the toilet—all telltale signs that I'm about to get a migraine.

Had I been more in my body and less engaged in the conversations in my head throughout the morning, I would have not only noticed the signals my body was sending, but I also would have been able to accurately interpret them. I would have taken better notice of the lack of sleep I'd had the night before and the hormonal triggers that were doing their best to send me telegrams warning of my impending (and debilitating) headache.

And because I hadn't paused to notice these signs earlier, I also knew I was about to pay the price.

It wasn't until I found the time and mental capacity to turn my attention inward and take a few long, deep breaths that I was able to flush some of the accumulated stress out of my body. As I sat, slowly inhaling and exhaling, details about the state of my body and mind began to rise to the surface of my awareness.

This is an easy technique we can all use any time. For example, as I write this paragraph, I can feel small vibrations in my arms. I'm also aware of my mind's desire to create a story about these sensations. The mindfulness work is to gently move back to the felt sensation and to observe different body parts as well as their rhythms.

Sitting here now, I notice the Excedrin I took for my migraine is starting to dull the pain in my head and that the tightness in my neck has migrated to my left side, and I become aware that my arms are resting above my heart.

The key to this kind of mindfulness technique is to allow yourself time to simply notice your sensations and allow them to be as they are. In doing so, you notice details: you perceive the nuances that are often overshadowed by other, more persistent physical sensations, and you gain a broader understanding of what's happening in your body. Having more information allows you to determine the best action—or lack of action—for the circumstances. And the more we do to nourish our body and observe its signals, the easier it becomes to live a happy, fulfilled life.

Embracing the Wisdom of the Body

Tapping into our physical experiences offers benefits both large and small. To begin with, we gain valuable insight about how our bodies function, which can make it easier to determine when our body is performing optimally or encountering a problem. We also become more adept at determining the source of our emotions.

This morning, had I taken a few moments to check in with my physical sensations, I would have been much quicker to figure out that my hormones were on fire, I was feeling tired, and I had inadvertently set the stage for a blockbuster migraine. Instead of allowing the frustration to build, I could have found an easy release valve—and would have had a much more pleasant, productive day.

Try as we might, we cannot control the appearance of our thoughts, feelings, and emotions. But, just like with tiny seeds, we can decide how to cultivate them. To do so, we first need to understand the relationship between thoughts, emotions, and our habits and beliefs. Thoughts are perhaps best understood as mental manifestations, often of perceptions or our interpretations of those perceptions.

Emotions, on the other hand, are the manifestations of feelings, such as anger, sadness, or happiness. Often, these feelings come with a physical manifestation in the body. If we're feeling frightened, we may notice that our hearts race, or we feel a jittery energy coursing through our bloodstream. If we're angry, we may notice a tightness in our chests or a seemingly uncontrollable desire to act.

Part of mindfulness is learning to identify how these emotions manifest in the body rather than simply acting upon them. If you're a visual learner, you may see that emotions arise as color: anger may feel like a bright, burning red; joy may feel like a golden halo encircling your head and heart.

Auditory learners may discover that emotion registers as a sound—maybe the delicate tinkle of a wind chime to indicate contentedness or discordant crashes to signal frustration. Kinesthetic learners may learn to identify feelings as bodily sensations—a tightness in your throat, a tingling in the extremities, an uncontrollable desire to dance while doing dishes in the kitchen.

As overwhelming as these feelings can seem at the moment, they are actually quite fleeting. In fact, left to their own devices, most feelings last only about ninety seconds on average. Take a feeling of fear or anger. Neuroscientist

Jill Bolte Taylor, author of *My Stroke of Insight,* explains it this way:

> Every reactivity is simply a group of cells performing their function. From the moment you have the thought that there's a threat and that circuit of fear gets triggered, it will stimulate the emotional circuitry related to it, which is the fight-or-flight reaction. That will trigger a physiological dumpage of usually norepinephrine or anger into the bloodstream. It will flush through you and flush out of you in less than ninety seconds, and the automatic response is over.

The problem, she cautions, is we rarely leave our emotional experiences to our body's automatic responses. Instead, we choose to persist with that emotional experience, often returning to the thought that first prompted the experience, thus creating a feedback loop that can make the emotion seem like it lasts a lot longer.[5]

By choosing to associate emotional responses with ideas and memories, we ultimately reinforce those connections, making them that much harder to break next time. Similarly, by choosing to ignore or shove down emotional experiences, we defer that experience and let it fester, which runs the risk of allowing it to become bigger and more impactful later.

That kind of re-remembering can take all kinds of forms. Have you ever, for instance, felt a kind of intuition about a person upon first meeting them? Perhaps you had a strong feeling of apprehension about them and did not know why. It could be intuition; however, it could also be a response to a stored memory you may not even remember making.

It could be you're not so much having a strong reaction to a particular person as you are, say, the perfume they are wearing, which also happens to be the perfume a harsh or insulting teacher might have worn when you were in grade school.

Our senses can imperceptibly move us in powerful ways. The taste of cardamom, which might be barely distinguishable in a loaf of raisin bread, can bring back loving memories of Easter with a cherished aunt. For the longest time, I couldn't figure out why I felt so happy (and excited) to buy things at T.J. Maxx until I finally realized they were playing all of my favorite dance songs from the 1980s.

An important part of mindfulness is remaining open and curious to these thoughts and the feelings and emotions they provoke. Understanding the felt sensations in your body allows you to preemptively choose how you are going to behave when an emotion is triggered; it also allows you the opportunity to assess whether you are responding based on habit, belief, or an accurately perceived threat.

Are you angry because of a memory or because of a situation that is valid in real time?

Some of my clients wonder, *If an emotion only lasts ninety seconds, how is it that I am still angry at someone who hurt me years ago?* That is a valid and important question. What I tell these clients is each time we think a thought, we reinforce a path in our brain. In time, what was just a few footsteps in the woods becomes a notable trail and, eventually, a road or even a superhighway.

Mindfulness allows us to recognize when we are being retriggered by an emotion like anger; it also allows us to invite our minds to feel something different and to recognize we are not in any present danger and don't need to act on that emotion.

Knowing how to recognize and feel that anger in our bodies is the first step in the process. And every time we choose to consciously make the switch to feeling and believing something other than anger, we are also laying down a new path in our brains; this more productive trail becomes stronger, and the older trail of anger and resentment becomes weaker.

To be clear: this kind of work requires conscious effort. It takes purposeful awareness to identify triggering thoughts and the resulting emotions in our body. It also draws upon our willpower to make the shift and decide what we are going to do with these thoughts and emotions.

If you haven't had enough sleep, if you had one too many glasses of wine, or if you just went on a sugar binge, it's going to be that much more difficult to dedicate yourself to an intentional practice of sifting through thoughts and emotions, identifying habits, beliefs, memories of past experiences, and making choices that are more aligned with your values and life purpose.

Mindfulness and self-care go hand in hand, and it's important to make time for the latter if you want to achieve the former.

That self-care can take many forms—and some you might not expect. For instance, twenty years ago, I found myself struggling to decide what my next career move would be. It was a period of real existential crisis for me: from the time I was ten years old, I had always worked for a living.

I grew up in a family of entrepreneurs, and both my father and my grandparents involved me in their businesses. I worked my way through college and eventually into a career I really loved. When I left that job in my early forties, I didn't know what to do next. I was far too young to retire, and even if I could have afforded to do so, I couldn't imagine not waking up to do work I valued.

Most mornings, I would wake up and immediately think, *What is my purpose? What am I supposed to be doing with myself?*

This deep, ongoing questioning felt like a lament. It seemed like there was always a weight on my shoulders, and I didn't know what to do next. What I did know was I needed help.

I knew from experience that talking to a therapist wasn't going to be the jolt I needed in this case. Instead, I needed to be pushed out of my comfort zone and compelled to hear other perspectives, especially those radically different from my own.

And so, I went online and found a women's retreat just across the border in Canada. I knew nothing about the facilitator, Grace Cirocco (who turned out to be a best-selling author and internationally renowned life coach), but I signed up anyway.

A week before the five-day retreat was scheduled to begin, I came down with an awful case of walking pneumonia. I was so sick I knew there was no way I could travel. I contacted Grace and explained my situation. *Annamarie, I will respect whatever decision you make,* she responded. *But I want to challenge you to consider that this is your body resisting a major change your brain knows it needs to make.* She encouraged me to come to the retreat anyway, and I eventually agreed.

At first, I was certain I'd made a mistake in attending. I was sharing a room with two other women and coughing constantly. I still felt awful, and I worried I was keeping my roommates awake at night. But in hindsight, I think the fact I was ill also made me more open to the content of the retreat and less likely to put up any protective barriers.

One of the instructions we received before arriving at the retreat was to bring a pillow. I had no idea why or what this pillow would be used for, so I just grabbed an old down pillow from the basement and packed it in my suitcase.

During the retreat, Grace asked us all to bring our pillows to a particular session, where we were also asked to sit in a circle on an intricate Oriental rug. The twenty of us were in a big room at the retreat center with dramatic vaulted ceilings and heavy wooden beams. It was lovely.

As I took in the scene, I also found myself wondering what would happen next and why we needed our pillows for this particular session. Eventually, Grace began talking about how important it is to allow ourselves to feel emotions and let them move around our bodies. She told us we were going to practice an exercise to help us with those emotions.

As she handed out little plastic wiffle ball bats, Grace explained that articulating our feelings while whacking our pillows would create an energetic release. Doing so would work on the whole body, including unblocking the throat and letting go of all the unspoken injustices, grievances, and anger.

When it was time to begin, I lightly tapped my pillow a few times with my bat—as if I didn't want to cause a scene. I was going through the motions of reciting past grievances, too, but I wasn't really buying into it. But then it occurred to me I really liked the feel of the bat in my hands. Even more, I liked the dull *thud* it made against my tired old pillow. With each little whack, I could feel my grip getting tighter and my strokes more definitive.

Then, before I knew it, I could feel the collective energy in the room growing more intense. Inside, my own anger was rising as well. I began wailing on that poor pillow and screaming as I did. The specifics of what I might have been saying were drowned out by the other twenty women, who by then were shouting as well.

I stayed in that moment until I realized just how much dust my bat was releasing from that dirty old pillow. If you know the character Pigpen from the *Peanuts*, you have an idea of what I'm talking about.

I started to feel self-conscious about the dust cloud I was creating. I looked around to see if anyone else had noticed.

They hadn't.

But Grace had noticed my self-consciousness and the look in her eyes told me she'd also seen how powerful a release I'd found before I became concerned about the dust. I'd found a valuable outlet for my pent-up emotions. And while I knew I would never have a career in pillow whacking, I also knew the physical release had been momentous.

When I returned home, I enrolled in a kickboxing course with a private trainer. Holy cow, you should have seen the look on my trainer's face when I went after a punching bag. I don't know if he wanted to audition me for a world tour or take out a restraining order.

But it didn't really matter. I had found the outlet I needed. The residual anger I'd been carrying around dissipated. New offenses no longer festered. I could feel the sense of betrayal from a former close friend belch out of me with a primal scream and a cloud of black, toxic gas. And then it was gone.

As a result, I felt lighter. Like a different person.

What I realize now is our brains are masterful at wishful thinking and obscuring the truth. Our bodies, however, almost always tell us how things really are. As psychologist Cordelia Fine puts it in her wonderful book, *A Mind of Its Own: How Your Brain Distorts and Deceives*, "Your brain is vainglorious. It's emotional and immoral. It deludes you. It is pigheaded, secretive, and weak-willed. Oh, and it's also a bigot."

As we'll discuss in more detail in the next couple of chapters, human brains have spent millennia trying to protect us by shielding us from anything that might be construed as unsafe, even if it's the truth.

The body, on the other hand, has no such aspirations. It can't help but be honest. While our brains are cycling around the same old stories, our bodies are often offering up new wisdoms and solutions. If we are willing to remain in an experience, notice our thoughts and emotions, as well as the felt sensations in our bodies, we can discover bigger, better pathways forward.

Finding those pathways begins with choosing to acknowledge the experience of emotions, however, they may manifest. Yes, that will mean learning to sit with uncomfortable experiences like fear and grief.

But it can be helpful to remember those uncomfortable experiences are just one side of the emotional coin. For every experience of grief also comes one of joy. With the other side of fear comes the kind of confidence and ease that allows you to throw your head back and laugh. Or to run down a hill, flapping your arms, and exulting in the experience of being alive.

Chapter 3 Takeaways

- Emotions come in a package: to experience happiness and joy, we must also be willing to experience grief and even anger. Mindfulness teaches us to make space for all emotions and to accept they are part of being human.

- Replacing judgment with curiosity allows us to experience emotions with our whole heart and to practice self-compassion.

- Our hearts, brains, and guts are interconnected and work together to create and process emotions through a complex network known as the gut-brain axis.

- A disrupted or upset digestive system can have a negative impact on our thoughts and feelings. Conversely, a healthy gut can help to regulate mood and improve our mental processes.

- A mindfulness practice encourages us to listen to our entire bodies and to glean what information different parts, systems, and even organs have to say about our overall well-being. That information allows us to make more intentional decisions that better serve us.

- Thoughts can be defined as the mental manifestations of our perceptions and ideas. Emotions, on the other hand, are the manifestations of our feelings. These feelings often declare themselves in physical ways, such as a tightness in the chest or seeing a bright color.

- Mindfulness enables us to more readily identify emotions and their manifestation in the body. By identifying and even naming these emotions, we create distance between them and our experience of them.

- Once we have identified an emotion, we can also choose to sit with that experience or to choose something different. For instance, if in a particular situation we identify we are angry, we can choose to sit and be curious about that experience; we can also choose to let it go and focus on a different experience. Making that switch, in turn, builds positive neurological connections.

Chapter 3 Exercises

Formal Mindfulness Practice

Traditional Body Scan

The purpose of this foundational practice is to cultivate the ability to notice what is being experienced in your body. It is designed to help you develop mindful awareness of your felt body sensations. If you adopt this practice, you may discover improved attention and mental agility, the ability to respond to situations more thoughtfully, improved sleep, and increased well-being.

This practice also supports the *informal* practices of mindfulness, such as eating with awareness, using the five senses to experience life more richly, and feeling emotions deeply without being swept away by them.

During this practice, I will guide you in shifting your attention through different parts of your body, encouraging you to notice sensations, or the lack of sensations, as you bring attention to each region of your body.

Although this body scan practice may ultimately result in relaxation, the intention is for you to have a direct experience of your body that leads you to deep awareness of the present moment and for you to cultivate curiosity, kindness, and non-judgment. This practice is about "falling awake" rather than falling asleep.

Let's begin.

Start this formal body awareness work by finding a safe place where you can practice uninterrupted. Align your body in a mindful posture, telling your body you're moving into a practice of deep awareness.

Find a comfortable position that reflects your intention to be alert yet relaxed in the practice. You may choose to lie down with your head supported and your arms resting at an angle at your sides. You may also stand, noticing your feet holding the weight of your body and your arms resting softly at your sides. Or you can sit in a chair or on a cushion and with your spine gently lifted toward the sky.

You may close your eyes or keep them open. If you choose closed, know you may open them at any point during the practice if that feels more supportive. You may also move or shift your body to find ease.

Allow your body now to rest in stillness and give yourself permission to experience this body scan with curiosity and kind awareness.

Take several long, deep breaths. Breathe in fully, and exhale slowly, in through your nose and out through your nose or mouth.

Begin to let go of noises around you and shift your attention from outside to inside, focusing on your breath. If you are distracted by sounds in the room, simply notice this and bring your focus back, returning your attention to your inhale and exhale.

Now, move your attention down to your feet, observing the sensations there. You might want to wiggle your toes or notice the sensations of your toes against your socks or shoes. Resist the temptation to judge what's happening as good or bad, right or wrong. And if you feel nothing, that's fine, too.

When you're ready, allow your attention to travel up your feet to your ankles, calves, knees, and thighs. Observe the sensations.

If your mind begins to wander, simply notice, knowing this is the mind doing what the mind does. You might even label it "wandering" and return your focus to the sensations in your legs. You may observe how sensations come and go, shift and change, and the impermanence of each sensation. Simply notice and allow the sensations to be in the moment, just as they are.

Then, on your next exhale, move your focus to the sensations in your lower back and pelvis. Possibly you sense your body softening and releasing as you breathe in and out. You might remind yourself, "There is nothing to fix here." Your breath and your felt sensations are exactly as they are at this moment.

Now, slowly move your attention up to your mid and upper back. You may become aware of sensations in your muscles, a temperature, or points of contact with furniture or the floor.

When you're ready, gently shift your focus to your stomach and your internal organs. You may feel your stomach expand on your inhale and let go with your exhale. Perhaps you notice the feeling of clothing or the vibration of digestion. If you notice opinions arising, gently let these go and return to noticing sensations.

As you continue to breathe, bring your awareness to your chest and heart region. You may notice the pulse and rhythm of your heartbeat, your chest rising and falling, or the feeling of your breath filling your lungs. Let go of thoughts or judgments that may arise.

On your next exhale, shift your focus to your hands and fingertips. Notice the sensations, vibrations, and temperature of your hands, the palms of your hands, and your fingers. If your mind wanders, gently bring it back to the sensations in your hands.

When you're ready, as you exhale, bring your awareness into your arms. Observe the sensations, or lack thereof, in your wrists, forearms, elbows, biceps, and triceps. You might notice differences between your left and right arms. As you exhale, you may also experience a softening and release of tension. Whatever you notice is fine.

Continue to breathe and shift the focus to your shoulder, neck, and throat. Simply place your attention on the sensations here. You may notice tension or ease, constriction or suppleness, strength or weakness. You may also notice the rise and fall of your shoulders moving along with your breath. Let go of the thoughts or stories that might pop into your awareness. Simply return your focus to your shoulder, neck, and throat.

And, on the next exhale, move your attention to your face, head, and scalp. Observe anything that wants to be noticed here. Possibly, you sense the movement of air as you breathe or a softening of your jaw and eyebrows. Gently fix your awareness on your face, head, and scalp.

And finally, when you're ready, let your attention and awareness expand out to include your entire body as a whole— from the crown of your head down to the tips of your toes. Feel the gentle rhythm of your breath as it moves through your body. Take as much time as you need here.

Now, as you come to the end of this practice, take a full, deep breath, taking in all the energy of this practice. Exhale that breath. Take another breath in, and let it out. When you're ready, wiggle your fingers and your toes and stretch in any way that feels supportive. If your eyes are closed, open them. Finally, send gratitude to your body for the ways it supports your movement and rest in this world.

Informal Mindfulness Practice

Listen to the Wind

This exercise was originally developed at Mind Body Align to help teachers lead mindfulness practices in the classroom. To engage younger learners, we also created a set of story-books depicting a butterfly named Tia, who finds shelter in a beautiful garden.

There, she makes friends with all kinds of critters, including grasshoppers, ants, bees, and caterpillars. She also learns about the practice of mindfulness from a wise old apple tree. One of the lessons Tree teaches Tia is how to listen to the W.I.N.D., an acronym for an informal mindfulness practice that helps people of all ages manage difficult emotions and situations.

This four-part practice can be used whenever you feel triggered. To begin,

W = **Wait a moment**: Stop what you're doing. Take a breath, and focus on your body.

I = **Investigate**: Do you sense anything in your body?

N = **Notice**: What are you feeling? What are you thinking?

D = **Do something!** Take action. Maybe you need to take a walk, talk to a friend, take a few deep breaths to calm your nervous system, make a list, or say something kind to yourself.

With this practice, you'll soon find that a triggering moment, desire, emotion, or experience will pass if you allow it to move through you like the wind.

···4···

The Science of Stress and Trauma (and how mindfulness helps to mitigate both)

WHEN I WAS growing up, my dad would drive me and my siblings to school every morning. At home, he was usually mild-mannered, but once he took his seat behind the wheel of a car, he became—well, easily excitable. He'd honk the horn; he'd admonish other drivers, and as a passenger, I definitely didn't want to talk to him.

It was the only aspect of his life where I ever saw him be aggressive, and in retrospect, I think driving was the one outlet my dad had to release his frustration about everything happening in the world. That kind of release had become a habit for him, to the point that I don't think he even realized he was doing it.

I have totally inherited this tendency. Sitting behind the wheel of a car is my power place; I really, really love aggressive, purposeful driving. If there's one thing that aggravates me, it's people in front of me driving slowly. Or when they don't put on their blinkers. Or if they refuse to get out of the left lane.

I have no tolerance for slow and inconsiderate people delaying my arrival to my next destination, and it doesn't take much until I'm frustrated to the point that I'm mumbling expletives and gripping the steering wheel with white knuckles. This aggravation is even worse if I'm feeling overscheduled (which happens a lot) or I haven't allowed enough time to get from point A to point B.

My husband and I live in a small town, and one of my real fears is that someday, someone I know is going to see me shouting all kinds of salty things as I pass them on a two-lane road. The problem is, I never think to remember that fear in the moment. Instead, I'm operating on sheer adrenaline and decades of habituated behavior. It's even worse if I haven't had enough sleep, if I haven't been eating well or exercising, or if I haven't found time to meditate.

When we experience stress, our body releases hormones that activate the sympathetic nervous system, a sophisticated neurological network that triggers our fight-or-flight response and allows us to respond to stressful situations in an instant. This response increases blood flow to essential muscles, heightens our mental awareness, and increases our physical strength, allowing us to perform strenuous—and even superhero—activities in an instant.

It's that response, for instance, that allows mothers to pull cars off of their trapped children or a hiker to outrun or battle a mountain lion bearing down upon them. The problem, of course, is that this stress response takes a toll on the body, increasing blood pressure, weakening the immune system, and causing digestive problems, including ulcers, especially if that stress is long-lasting.[1]

By engaging in regular self-care, we can minimize the appearance of stress hormones and their impact on the body. In addition to getting enough sleep, eating well, and meditating, other techniques include staying hydrated, spending time in nature, moving your body in a way that keeps you feeling flexible and strong, and engaging in activities that feel purposeful.

These kinds of activities result in immediate, positive physical changes, including lowering your blood pressure and heart rate, increasing feel-good hormones like dopamine, and calming your breathing.[2] Understanding the science behind why this works—and what you can do to manage your stress, its root causes, and its manifestation—will go a long way toward maintaining a mindful life that exemplifies your goals and ideals.

The Place Where Trauma Lives

Although parts of our brains have evolved in a way that enabled our species to develop language, culture, and technology, other parts of our brains have remained largely unchanged. Certain basic responses are hardwired into the human brain, and that primitive part of the brain functions as if we were living as tribes of hunters and gatherers who are responding to stress stimuli in the same way, whether we are in immediate physical danger or facing a hard deadline at work.

That's in large part because of the sympathetic nervous system, a powerful neurological network that triggers our fight, flight, or freeze responses and allows us to respond to stressful situations.

Here's how it works: each time we experience fear, our bodies begin to secrete adrenaline, a hormone that causes our heart to beat faster and our blood vessels to route blood to our organs and key muscle groups, making us both more alert and ready to take on herculean physical challenges.

Adrenaline also increases our blood sugar, ensuring we have more energy to confront whatever challenge awaits while also tamping down our nervous system's ability to process pain so we'll keep at that challenge, even when the going gets tough.

Meanwhile, it also tells our brain to shift its operating system from the logic-driven frontal cortex to the amygdala, which is responsible for identifying threats and shifting us into fight-flight-freeze mode. Along the way, it overshadows our brain's capacity for creativity, introspection, and even rational thinking.

On the contrary, the amygdala wants us only to focus on escaping (or destroying) an immediate threat. That's just one reason psychologists refer to this state as the "amygdala hijack": this tiny part of our brain literally takes over and begins driving the bus.

That's all fine and good when confronted with a saber tooth tiger or a very real contemporary threat, like an intruder in our home or the prospect of being mugged. However, the amygdala can also prevent us from accurately assessing dangers and making good choices. It has little interest in rational thinking, sound judgment, or the consequences of our actions. Moreover, prolonged time in the fight-flight-freeze response can leave us overstimulated, fatigued, and more susceptible to both mental and physical ailments.

To see the amygdala in action, you don't need anything as dramatic as a major accident or natural disaster. Instead, just find the nearest teenager and take a peek at their world. Cognitive researchers now know that most teenagers are, in fact, part (or evenly mostly) lizard until they're about 25, which is when the rational part of their brain begins to hold its own against the amygdala.

In the meantime, hair-trigger responses, impulsive choices, and sometimes decidedly bad decision-making is the norm. And if you've ever asked a teenager *why* they decided to eat their weight in hot dogs, take a car for a joyride, or cut classes to attend a rave, they may well tell you they have no idea. That's not because they're avoiding the question; it's because they honestly didn't give it a second (or even a first) thought at the time.[4]

And let's be honest: few of us fully escape our lizard selves, regardless of our age. The amygdala is always up there, looking for danger, and poised to act. When it does, it can turn off the thinking, logical parts of our brain so we can react quickly and without logically processing first or taking time for careful consideration.

Knowing your amygdala's preferred behavior in that situation is a helpful part of the mindfulness journey. In some people, for instance, the body may respond by entering a state of immobility or "freezing," in which the person becomes very still and quiet, often with a reduced heart rate and breathing rate.

This is totally me.

My reaction to large amounts of stress is to freeze like an opossum or do my best to make myself invisible. Conversely, some people become like MacGyver from the 1980s TV show, *MacGyver*. They use their knowledge, creativity, and problem-solving skills to come up with innovative solutions to difficult problems, often using limited resources.

They have an increase in cognitive function that may be due to a variety of factors, including increased blood flow and oxygenation to the brain, the release of certain neurotransmitters that enhance cognitive function, and increased energy and attention that can improve focus and concentration. My husband fits easily into this category. In the face of high-stress situations, his complex cognitive processing moves into high gear, and he becomes the hero, the problem solver, the man with a plan.

Our primitive brain has remained hardwired for social interaction as well. It wasn't too long ago in human history that getting kicked out of the tribe could mean a sure death. Living in a community allowed individuals to share resources and tasks, making sure basic needs like food, shelter, and security were met.

Most of us no longer need a tribe to stay alive, but our desire for social interaction has remained an intrinsic part of our identity, and research has shown that social isolation and rejection can have adverse effects on mental and physical health as well as cognitive function.[5] That's because our brains have evolved to privilege a sense of belonging, which means we can't help but worry about how other people perceive us.

We fear rejection; we need to know we're in good standing with those around us. Our bodies have a physical reaction when we think we've wronged or offended someone. These feelings of guilt or shame, in turn, can trigger the release of stress hormones and activate the sympathetic nervous system, ultimately preparing us for a real or perceived battle.

Compare these evolutionary responses to our modern reality, a world where social media interactions involve thousands of people you may have never met and include body language that is distorted on virtual calls and meetings. The specific impact of these virtual interactions and lack of social cues on mental health is not well understood; however, it stands to reason it has some influence on the increase of mental illness, suicide, and stress-related diseases.

I suspect one major contributing factor is the fact that we rarely have the ability to assess our standing in a community, whether it's a local or global one. We have a brief interaction with someone via Zoom and then don't have the opportunity to see or interact with them again for weeks, months, or sometimes ever. If we feel we may have wronged them, there is no discreet way to assess that feeling, no probability of running into them at the village well or while doing laundry at the river, no moments when casual conversation could provide the necessary clues about their feelings.

The effect of all of this can feel like nothing short of crazy-making—and for very good reason. As a recent study in the *Journal of American Medicine* reveals, even the perception of stress is enough to negatively impact cognitive performance in real ways.[6] In the short term, that can mean impaired memory function, an inability to self-assess (and self-regulate!), exaggerated emotional responses, and poor impulse control.

Long-term, this stress can lead to dementia, Alzheimer's, and other degenerative cognitive impairments. It also compromises the body's immune system, making us more susceptible to viruses and some diseases.[7]

Happily, mindfulness provides an effective way for us to regain control of the wheel. Even exercises as simple as a body scan or circle breathing can be enough to shift our brains from a sympathetic nervous system response to one favoring a parasympathetic nervous system, the so-called "rest and digest" hardwiring that returns our body's systems to a state of rest.[8]

Under the control of the parasympathetic nervous system, our heart rate slows, and our blood pressure lowers. Our breathing slows and takes less energy. Our digestive tract begins to work normally again, processing food into the sugars our cells need to do their jobs.

As all of these systems stand down from a code red state, our brain also hands control back to our frontal cortex, allowing us to more accurately assess and respond to whatever stimuli is before us. That allows us to continue on the path toward happiness and self-regulation discussed in Chapter 2.

Given how powerfully our bodies can express themselves, why are so many of us disconnected from that experience? For some people, the answer is clear: they've experienced a serious threat to their life or a trauma that resulted in a physiological change and literal disengagement with the body.

From a psychological perspective, it can just feel safer to distance yourself from your bodily experience, especially if that body was the site of the actual trauma. Sexual assault survivors, veterans who served in violent combat, and other people managing post-traumatic stress disorder have spoken powerfully about how difficult it can feel to remain connected with their body after a scarring incident.[9]

It doesn't even take a major traumatic event for people to feel dislocated in their body—or for the body to catch us off guard. Years ago, I made a major change from a successful career in interior design to a job working in historic building restoration. When I began that transition, I didn't realize how much of my identity had been wrapped up in my career as an interior designer.

Without realizing it, I had let it begin to define my every waking moment—and plenty of my sleeping ones, too. Once I left that position and it no longer consumed the lion's share of my mental energy and emotions, I began to feel as if I were floating—and not in a good way. I'd lost my anchor, and consequently, I had nothing with which to ground myself.

Needless to say, it wasn't a comfortable feeling. I began to cast around in search of a project that could give me a sense of purpose and an outlet for all this extra time and energy. For reasons I still don't understand, I settled upon a triathlon.

To understand just how out of character this was for me, you should know up until that time my only real fitness regime consisted of walking around my neighborhood or occasionally racing after geese in the backyard. Nevertheless, I threw myself wholeheartedly into training for that race: I bought a guidebook and hired a private swim coach (one tiny hitch in my otherwise perfect plan was I didn't really know how to swim). I also signed up for spin classes three times a week, thinking that would prepare me for the cycling portion of the race.

The spin classes were held at our local YMCA. Before each class, the instructor would arrange the stationary bikes into a U shape and place his bike at the top of the U. I always chose a bike in the back, thinking I'd escape the notice of other class members.

I loved that spin class and how it inspired me to push my limits. But here's the thing: every time I began to really exert myself, I would also begin crying. And not just a few tears. No, I'm talking a full-on, heaving, hiccupping, sobbing emotional release. Whoever happened to be on the bike next to me would invariably respond with something like horror or an impulse to call 911.

As for me, I was mostly just perplexed by my response.

In hindsight, I shouldn't have been. As a yoga instructor, I know this kind of emotional response can happen when people take to the mat. Certain postures like a twist, hip opener, or even just a deep stretch will release emotional stress and tension that people may not have even known they had. It can be surprising and even unsettling when it happens to us, but there are real benefits to that release.

I still don't know what it was about the stationary bike that set off my release. But I did always feel better after it happened. That's because, oftentimes, stress and trauma need a physical way to exit the body.

That said, it's also important to note that confronting and releasing trauma is a powerful experience, made exponentially so by the severity of the trauma. If you are working through chronic or complex trauma, such as an adverse childhood experience, beginning to unpack it can feel so debilitating you can literally start to wonder if you'll survive. No one should go through that experience alone.

If you think you might be suffering from PTSD or are even just bearing the weight of a past traumatic event, it is a very good idea to work with a trained mental health professional or psychotherapist. They can provide important tools to help you manage the emotions and feelings sparked by unpacking your past.

If, on the other hand, you are a person who feels you can safely tackle your healing on your own, mindful movement can be a great practice to include in a healing regimen. For starters, it can funnel emotional trauma out of the body without your mind having to consciously recall or relive the traumatic event itself. Mindfulness movement is also an excellent way to center yourself and to prevent injury.

Take that spin class of mine. Once I got past all the dramatic weeping, I began to focus on my body, observing my legs moving the pedals, feeling the sensations in my muscles, tendons, and bones. I noticed my heart beating faster and my breath moving in and out of my body as I became more aware of how my muscles and joints were performing.

This level of awareness not only helped me to process latent emotions; it also made me less likely to injure myself whenever on a bike. The same is true for activities like trail running, rock climbing, and surfing; intentionally focusing on the body as it performs a strenuous activity can both keep you balanced and help prevent injury.

We have all experienced some kind of trauma in our lives. Maybe it's breaking your arm falling out of a tree as a young child. Maybe it's being bullied for looking different than other kids. Perhaps you are the survivor of a car accident, a natural disaster, or an abusive relationship. The body records trauma in ways we are only beginning to understand.

Researchers also now believe our cells inherit trauma from previous generations. Referred to as intergenerational or epigenetic trauma, this inheritance can literally change how our genes function.

Descendants of a famine survivor, for instance, may be more prone to obesity or diabetes; those of a holocaust survivor may have a higher likelihood of developing clinical depression or heart disease. Researchers believe this happens because parents who are trauma victims pass down cellular differences to their children, particularly where stress hormones like cortisol are concerned.[10]

Inherited or not, the body records trauma. As noted psychiatrist Bessel van der Kolk writes in his international best-seller, *The Body Keeps the Score,* trauma imprints itself on our minds and bodies, changing our physiology and our hormonal responses and interfering with our ability to be present in any given moment. After a traumatic incident, the brain can actually rewire its own alarm system, making us feel hypervigilant and more prone to panic, even when there is no perceivable threat.

But as van der Kolk also explains, we can rewire those impulses and heal the scars trauma has left behind.

There are multiple ways to heal the effects of trauma on the body and the mind. Medication is one. Talk therapy is another. Both can be highly effective modalities for helping individuals work through past events and find a new sense of wholeness.

Increasingly, though, psychologists are turning to the mind-body connection as an effective means of healing. Beginning in the 1970s, world-renowned trauma researcher Peter Levine began introducing trauma victims and their health practitioners to the concept of somatic experiencing, or a body-oriented approach to processing trauma.

These experiences can range from simple breathing exercises to running water over your hands to ecstatic dancing—anything that gives the body an opportunity to continue processing a past traumatic event.[11]

Another powerful tool is eye movement therapy, also known as *eye movement desensitization and reprocessing* or EMDR. Unlike traditional talk therapy, EMDR employs our eye's natural movements to help patients process traumatic events. A therapist will move their fingers or a pointer back and forth while asking the patient to follow these motions with their eyes. The patient is then asked to recall a past traumatic event and the physical sensations associated with it.

The idea here is the natural movements of our eyes help the brain to reprocess the event in a more productive way. Just as our ancient ancestors would scan the horizon, looking for threats in the form of saber tooth tigers or rival tribes, so too can our contemporary eyes use that motion to assure us of our safety. That eye movement from right to left (what scientists call "bilateral" eye movement) helps the brain break a large and painful memory into smaller pieces, which in turn become more accessible, more manageable to process, and ultimately easier to heal.[12]

As mindfulness practitioners, we can achieve similar effects on our own by simply taking a few moments to slowly scan a room: the gradual, back-and-forth movement of the eyes has a noticeable calming effect on many people. Walking, hiking, and other outdoor experiences achieve similar benefits (along with the added plus of fresh air and beautiful scenery).[13]

As a proof of concept, consider the story of a close friend of mine who developed PTSD while deployed in the Middle East. After returning to the States, she joined a hiking group with other veterans. There, she discovered that the act of scanning the trail in front of her while hiking was a great way to process past events in a safe and productive way. In fact, it was so beneficial to her that she decided to hike the entire 2200-mile Appalachian Trail, the 1200-mile Pacific Northwest Trail, and, as I'm writing this, she is hiking the 2653-mile Pacific Crest Trail as well.

Today, multiple nonprofit organizations, such as Wounded Warrior Project, help to get veterans suffering from PTSD outside and on trails, rivers, and other nature-based recreation opportunities, where using their bodies allows them to process and recover from trauma.

Looking back, I can see I was undertaking my own somatic experience in that spin class. I may not have been conscious that my mind was processing past events, but the simple act of engaging specific muscles and focusing on that act allowed me to touch emotions buried deep within my body.

Given that experience, I've since looked for similar opportunities, such as therapeutic yoga classes. These, along with other trauma-informed mindfulness experiences, work to slowly increase body awareness in a way that feels safe for participants. This can help to toggle between the sympathetic and parasympathetic nervous systems, which also creates a greater sense of emotional and physical safety.

By using our bodies to learn more about our minds and the experiences they store, we not only strengthen the mind-body connection, but we also gain new insight and ownership of our emotional experience. This contributes to greater self-love and an overall heightened sense of well-being.

Participants in trauma-informed activities such as yoga and meditation report an increase in confidence, happiness, and peaceful feelings. They find they're more able to stay in the present moment and to acknowledge their thoughts and feelings without judgment. That allows for greater patience—both for oneself and for others.

As one participant in a trauma-informed yoga program told researchers, "I feel more authentic than I ever have."[14] *That's* the real power of using mindfulness to reroute our body's response to stress.

The beautiful part of this kind of experience is it occurs largely without conscious thought, so our brains are less likely to hook onto the story of trauma and strengthen previously held narratives. Instead, we're moving the trauma through our body without reigniting it or the feelings and emotions associated with it.

Whether you opt for a kinesthetic experience like yoga, an EMDR-based wilderness experience, or a more cognitively focused mindfulness exercise, such as meditation or a body scan, remember the benefits arise not from how well you perform the activity but from their ability to make you feel more grounded and comfortable with your emotional experience.

Chapter 4 Takeaways

- The sympathetic nervous system is the part of our brain and body that responds to stress. Once activated, it releases powerful hormones that prepare our body for dangerous situations and stimulates the fight-flight-freeze response.

- A mindfulness practice can help you understand whether you are someone who tends to fight, flee, or freeze in situations. Understanding which of these responses you tend to exhibit can help you become more conscious of how stress manifests in your body and mind.

- Because human beings have also evolved as tribal or pack animals, any perception of rejection can not only create powerful feelings of guilt or shame but can also trigger the sympathetic nervous system and associated stress hormones.

- Stress and its associated hormones can lead to negative mental and physical effects, including cognitive impairment, high blood pressure, and a weakened immune system.

- Mindfulness also helps minimize stress and allows us to tap into our parasympathetic, or "rest and digest," nervous system.

- In addition to the sympathetic and parasympathetic nervous systems, human brains have also evolved to cultivate a sense of belonging and a fear of rejection, which often manifest in the physical body and activate the sympathetic nervous system.

- Both the body and mind record trauma, which can not only change our physiology but can also rewire the brain, making us more prone to anxiety, panic, and stress.

- Whether great or small, traumatic incidents can also weaken the mind-body connection and hamper our ability to feel in touch with our physical selves and sensations.

- Trauma can be passed down from generation to generation through what is known as epigenetic or intergenerational trauma.

- Mindful movement is a powerful way to rebuild the mind-body connection. Walking meditation, restorative yoga, EMDR, and even hiking or cycling can be very effective ways to process trauma and build a more holistic sense of self.

- If you are someone who has experienced profound trauma or lingering PTSD, it is advisable to process that trauma with a trained therapist or other healthcare professional.

Chapter 4 Exercises

Formal Mindfulness Practice

Walking Meditation

Walking meditation is a great way to practice mindfulness, especially if you are someone who gets fidgety when sitting still or are looking to inhabit your body more fully. As the great mindfulness teacher and philosopher Thich Nhat Hanh once wrote, walking meditation is an opportunity to feel grounded and nourished and to express reverence both for our bodies and for the planet on which we live.

To practice walking meditation, begin by choosing a place that feels peaceful and safe to you (i.e., an outdoor space like a beach or park or any place in your own home). The specific location doesn't matter. All places, after all, have the potential to be sacred and special.

To help you stay present, set a timer or alarm on your phone or watch. I recommend beginning with ten minutes if you are new to the practice.

Once you've set your timer, begin by taking very slow, deliberate steps. Focus on the feeling of your feet on the floor or the earth: is it cold? Warm? Soft? Hard? Slowly raise and step forward with one foot, paying close attention as first your heel lifts and then the rest of your foot. Gently set that foot down before beginning with the next. Remember: the aim here is to go slowly and to make small, deliberate movements.

For some people, this act of paying attention to each step is enough. If you choose, you can also coordinate your breathing and your steps. For instance, Thich Nhat Hanh recommends taking one breath with each step; he also suggests focusing on your exhale by taking one or two steps with each in breath, followed by two or three steps with each out breath.

You might also consider incorporating a mantra as part of this practice. You might choose to repeat something like "My body is strong," or "I give thanks for these legs," or "Breathing in, I feel connected to my body. Breathing out, I feel connected to the Earth."

Informal Mindfulness Practice

Modified Body Scan

One of the great things about mindfulness is it can be practiced anytime, anywhere. This is especially true when we are looking to build our mind-body connection. I like to use moments when I am waiting in line or for an appointment as an opportunity for informal practice.

For instance, when standing in line at the grocery store, use that time to observe your body, beginning with the position of your feet and working upwards. Are you favoring one foot over the other? How is your posture? What does the basket or cart feel like in your hands? Do you notice any stress or tightness? Soreness or tenderness? If so, take a moment to thank your body for everything it does and send it healing, nurturing energy.

This is also a *great* practice for some of life's more annoying experiences, such as waiting while in line at the DMV or passing through airport security.

··· 5 ···

Shoulda, Woulda, Coulda: The (Unhelpful) Stories Our Brains Tell Us

I'VE ALWAYS THOUGHT of myself as a peacekeeper: the person who could smooth over any situation and de-escalate whatever conflict came my way. As a high school senior, I actually won the award for being the kindest member of our graduating class. That award really cemented my own sense of personal identity.

In fact, I'd so internalized this role over the years that *compassionate peacekeeper* became a major part of how I identified myself. You can imagine, then, how disorienting and unsettling it was when that role was called into question by my new mindfulness practice.

As a beginner, I spent a lot of time learning to pay attention to my thoughts. I have to admit: it was a shocking experience. Prior to my mindfulness journey, I had no idea how judgmental I could be or how much of my mental energy was dedicated to critical thoughts.

For years, I had walked through the world with a smile on my face and a soothing tone to my voice. But all the while, the back of the house was awash in corrosive, judgmental, and inflexible thoughts—a darker, more discontented version of me. I really didn't like this Negative Nellie. And I definitely didn't want to spend time with her.

Nevertheless, the more time I committed to my mindfulness practice, the more present she seemed to be—and the less control over her I seemed to have. Very quickly, I went from being the person who was always sweet and nice to a woman who was willful, obstinate, and short-tempered.

For the first time in my life, every time I felt a strong, challenging emotion, I was allowing myself to fully feel and express it. But because I was new to this way of being, I didn't really have any idea about effective ways to communicate what I was feeling, nor did I have the skills to set compassionate boundaries for myself and others.

I gradually began to realize I'd never developed the skill set necessary to release my overwhelming emotions in a productive way. Consequently, all these newfound feelings and sentiments had a way of tumbling out—and sometimes in explosive or exceedingly messy ways.

That all came to a head one holiday weekend. For years, my husband and I hosted a clambake at our lake house every Labor Day. We'd invite all our friends and family, and typically, about seventy or so people would show up. There was always a lot of activity on this particular weekend: lawn games and water skiing, a constant stream of food for people of all ages.

It was controlled chaos.

To keep my sanity, I had a couple of ground rules. One of them was that guests were welcome to spend the night, but they needed to do so in a tent outside. This allowed me to invest 100 percent of my energy into the day, knowing after the lights went out, I could rest.

I also asked guests to pay close attention to their children and to leave their pets at home. With the lake nearby and a dangerous road close as well, watching children was a life-or-death necessity. The idea of keeping tabs on dogs as well was just more stress than I could manage. However, with those two rules in place, I could usually let go of any anxiety or frustration and simply enjoy the weekend.

One particular year, some close friends of ours attended the clambake and brought their new chihuahua puppy—an adorable, teeny little dog, literally the cutest thing you've ever seen. But he was also a typical puppy, which meant he hadn't been fully house-trained and was especially prone to accidents when he was excited.

As soon as he arrived, the puppy began racing around the house. Every time I stepped inside, I found a new piddle spot on the floor. Meanwhile, another guest had brought their tween daughter, who promptly planted herself on my sofa with a dripping chocolate ice cream cone in her hand. As I watched the girl try unsuccessfully to manage the cone, I couldn't help but imagine how quickly the dark brown ice cream could cascade down onto the sofa's light tweed fabric.

I tried persuading the tween to take her ice cream cone outside, where she could enjoy the beautiful weather and not worry about making a mess, but she wasn't having any of it. Because I don't have children of my own, I'm not very practiced in the art of reasoning with a headstrong child. I tried again to persuade her to go outside but to no avail.

So now I had a dog piddling all over the house, a child I couldn't control, and the threat of irreparable damage to a favorite piece of furniture. Meanwhile, outside were seventy or so guests whom I was supposed to be entertaining. I could feel my frustration building.

And then it began to rain.

Accompanied by my husband, a few of our guests came inside and announced they planned to sleep in the basement and not their tents. The previous Annamarie would have just smiled and agreed. A balanced and centered Annamarie would have maybe taken her husband aside and said, *Sweets, this isn't acceptable. Allowing these guests to sleep downstairs is breaking one of my primary rules.*

Needless to say, I did neither of those things. Instead, I decided to let myself be angry. *Really* angry. The temper tantrum that followed was definitely not one of my proudest moments.

Around the same time as this disastrous weekend, I also began to notice how quickly I'd begun to flare up at work. Previously, I'd never let people see me frustrated if projects weren't completed properly or on time. Now, it seemed like I snapped at the drop of a hat.

I loathed this new version of "work me." I didn't want to be judgmental or negative; I definitely didn't want to be curt or hurtful in my word choice and tone. The fact that I was now doing all of this and more sent me into a shame spiral. The more annoyed or irritable I sounded, the more critical I became of myself.

The more critical I became of myself, the more frustrated and upset I sounded. I kept hearing these negative voices in my head, and try as I might, I couldn't silence them. It was maddening.

But then I remembered a simple yet profound quote from mindfulness expert Jack Kornfield: "Thoughts think themselves." In that moment, I realized I didn't have to embody all these "negative" thoughts and feelings, and I certainly didn't need to let them define me.

Instead, I could just watch my critiques come and go. That, in turn, would allow me to treat both the thoughts and myself with compassion. I could let go of the idea that I'm a terrible person and recognize that my subconscious brain was doing what it's been programmed to do.

The great self-inquiry teacher Byron Katie, author of *The Work*, has also written extensively about this phenomenon. She encourages her readers to be curious about the notions they've accepted as facts, as well as the beliefs they have about the world, other people, and themselves.

Two of the questions she encourages people to consider include: "Is this true?" and "How do I know it's true?" Those two queries can go a long way toward stopping destructive self-talk.

If you are someone who can easily get hijacked by a critical and judgy internal monologue telling you you're a bad person, pausing the monologue long enough to ask yourself if that self-recrimination is justified can be a powerful moment of self-awareness.

Take the clambake at our lake house: After I lost my temper, I could have easily given myself over to self-recrimination and persuaded myself I'm actually not a nice or kind person. After all, surely anyone worthy of the "kindest senior" award in high school doesn't lose her temper at puppies, children, and soggy houseguests, right? By following Byron Katie's model, I found a way to contextualize these responses without letting them define me.

Mindfulness gives us the tools to perform this kind of contextualization in real-time. Say I let myself go down a shame spiral and eventually arrive at the conclusion that I am, in fact, a mean and terrible person.

If I follow Byron Katie's lead, my next task would be to dig deep and ask myself if it's actually true I'm not a good person. I might even succeed in concluding that, yes, I'm just plain awful. But that's where the brilliance of Katie's second question, which includes a subtle switch in language, comes in: *How do I know it's true that I'm a bad person?*

I could try answering that question with the example of my outburst at the party; I could even add in the time I snapped at one of my team members when she was late delivering a project. However, even the most self-critical version of me would probably notice these situations had less to do with my overall character than they did with my triggered response to certain situations.

Faced with the conclusion that I may, in fact, be a good person who sometimes loses her temper or whose monkey brain sometimes impersonates a Negative Nellie, I'd have no choice but to reassess this story I'd been telling myself about my overall worth (or lack thereof).

As much as we'd like to believe that mindfulness makes us sainted individuals, the fact remains that it more often allows us to acknowledge our humanness, which means we must also acknowledge our faults, foibles, and weaknesses.

The trick, of course, to avoid assigning value or any kind of narrative importance to our humanness. In place of calling these aspects of our character "bad," we can use them as opportunities to develop compassion for ourselves and others and to give ourselves the grace we need to live happier, more forgiving lives.

Asleep at the Wheel: How Habits Keep Us on Autopilot

Since time immemorial, philosophers have debated the nature of consciousness. Today, there are several major schools of thought on the subject. One theory, held by scholars Michael Graziano and David Rosenthal, is that consciousness is generated by chemical reactions in our brains that do not require us to actively make any interpretations.[3]

In other words, we don't have to recognize thoughts or read our own minds for these conscious thoughts to exist. I find this theory fascinating, particularly the idea that we can make decisions without conscious thought or the awareness of memory. Instead, we can subsist on what philosophers call *the illusion of immediacy:* thoughts and feelings appear in our minds because of chemical reactions and autonomic (i.e. involuntary) responses in our brains rather than because of anything deliberate or intentional.

We believe we are making conscious choices when those decisions and judgments are actually being made by our habits and beliefs and without any agency on our part. This idea is aptly encapsulated by the Jack Kornfield expression, "Thoughts think themselves." Just as the salivary glands secrete saliva, so too does the mind think thoughts—and often with no more emotion than other involuntary bodily actions.

If you're like me, you'll find a real sense of freedom and liberty in this theory. On more than a few occasions, I've been embarrassed, disappointed, or frustrated by some of my thoughts. At times, they've seemed petty, unfair, or even mean. In extreme cases, they have led me to think I'm a terrible person.

Understanding I have only so much control over these thoughts was a game-changer. Rather than constantly evaluating my thoughts as good or bad, I could begin merely observing them as something other than myself. Looking at my thoughts from a nonjudgmental perspective, I could begin to understand where they were influenced by long-held beliefs, my culture, and even my own genetics.

I began to realize many of these thoughts weren't even mine—they were the product of generations of experience and ideologies. They were based on lessons, right or wrong, that I'd been taught as a child. They arose out of observations I'd made in society or while consuming media. Understanding that those thoughts had been passed down to me allowed me to foster self-compassion and understanding.

The same is true for those thoughts we don't even consciously register. For instance, have you ever driven all the way to work or dropped off your little ones at school, only to arrive with the realization that you have no idea how you got there? Presumably, you obeyed stop signs and traffic lights, and you somehow managed to avoid colliding with other vehicles.

Nevertheless, you arrived at your destination with no conscious memory of any of it. Known as driver inattentiveness or highway hypnosis, this lack of conscious awareness is so common that reams of scholarly articles have been written on the subject. What psychologists have found is that driver inattentiveness most often occurs because we're traveling the same route out of habit rather than conscious intention.

As a result, we allow our brains to put the driving on autopilot while we map out the rest of our day or replay an argument we had with our spouse at the breakfast table. In both instances, our brains are focused on the future, the past, or judgments about what's happening during the drive rather than the present moment.[1]

In my own life, I've often found that this kind of inattentiveness arises because I allow my brain to concoct all kinds of stories that may or may not have any basis in reality.

For example, I might be running late for a meeting when I get stuck behind a woman driving the speed limit (the audacity!). In no time, I'll get myself worked up, thinking about the people I'm going to inconvenience by showing up late or my mother's admonishments when I was a child about how important it is to always be prompt.

Instead of reflecting upon my lack of good time management or the low stakes of arriving a few minutes late, I'll blame the law-abiding driver for my tardiness. Suddenly, I've become the victim in a narrative where this innocent stranger is out to get me.

By the time I arrive at my destination, I'm super-agitated: angry at the unknown woman, embarrassed I've kept people waiting, ashamed I once again managed to overschedule myself. Along the way, what started as a few choice words muttered under my breath has morphed into a dramatic one-act play with yours truly as the tragic heroine.

Why? Because I have habituated myself to respond this way.

However, if I take the time to pause and reflect in these situations, I will also begin to identify what's happening behind the scenes in my subconscious mind. For instance, as a substitute for working myself up into a state of shame, I might take the opportunity to gently chide myself for again overpacking my schedule. I also might smile at the welcome memories of my dad behind the wheel and remember this propensity for mild road rage is an ingrained habit.

In both instances, I also have the opportunity to remind myself I can choose something different. That process of going from being triggered to experiencing nostalgia and curiosity can be launched with acts of attentiveness as simple as noticing my hands on the steering wheel, feeling my foot on the gas pedal, or looking around and taking notice of the world around me.

As individuals, each of us sees the world in our own unique way and through the filter of everything that has happened to us up until that point. We've stored memories and ideas about particular ways of doing things, as well as the results those methods produced.

If our parents gave into our temper tantrums when we were young, we might expect that a similar display of emotionality would allow us to get our way as adults. If, on the other hand, we were taught to never rock the boat, we might find ourselves particularly uncomfortable about the prospect of offering negative feedback or taking issue with someone's behavior.

The same is true for our dispositions and beliefs as well. How influential people in our lives modeled their responses to everything from failures and accomplishments to love or rejection all factor into the lens through which we view the world. And regardless of our backgrounds, we've all become practiced in attaching less meaning to some things and more meaning to others. As a result, we all have our own perspective on this thing we call "reality."

And that perspective is directly related to the habits we've formed along the way.

Happily, mindfulness helps us identify how our previous thoughts and experiences cause us to filter new information, sensations, and feelings. To begin this process, it's helpful to consider the very nature of a habit. I like to define a habit as "an action that you perform repeatedly without needing to be mindful—or even all that conscious—about doing it."

In other words, a habit is something you've done so many times you literally don't need to think about it anymore. A great example is brushing your teeth. If you're like me, you automatically perform this activity the same way, no matter where you are or what day it is.

Mindfulness encourages us to do something even as mundane as this act of personal hygiene with more intention. Several years ago, I attended a talk by a noted mindfulness teacher who said if you want an easy exercise in mindfulness, brush-your teeth with your non-dominant hand and focus on the associated feelings this switcheroo prompts, both physically as well as mentally and even emotionally.

Are you more aware of the feel of the brush in your hand or the motion required to get your teeth clean? Does the visual perception of yourself in the mirror become more or less pronounced than it would otherwise? Does focusing your attention on this new way of brushing encourage your mind to construct stories or assign value?

There's no right or wrong answer here: just observe the thoughts and feelings this shift in your routine prompts, as well as any sneaky attempts your mind might be attempting to forge meaning out of these observations.

Another reason I like this exercise so much is it also demonstrates just how different things feel when we make deliberate choices, rather than allowing habits to keep us on autopilot. Being curious in this way is a great way to practice mindfulness.

It's particularly effective in this case because brushing your teeth is an ingrained habit, which frees up your brain to focus on other things and distracts us from the moment at hand. Making a conscious choice to perform a task differently interrupts that habituated response and offers an opportunity to return to the present.

And that's the thorny thing about habits: they often let us take the easy way out of a situation. However, "easy" doesn't always—or even often—serve us. For instance, you might have fallen into the habit of usually eating dessert after dinner or opening a bottle of wine while you're cooking.

There's nothing inherently wrong with a cookie or a nice glass of chardonnay, of course. Consuming either—or both—every night, on the other hand, is a surefire way to establish habits that don't serve us (and undoubtedly lead to extra calories we probably don't need).

Of course, if you've ever attempted "Dry January," the month of no drinking, or "Whole 30," a month of no drinking along with no sugar, grains, dairy, or processed food, you know how difficult it can be to break an otherwise benign-seeming habit.

Why is that? Simple brain chemistry, as it turns out.

Say you have a habit of eating chocolate around 3 p.m. each day in an attempt to stave off a mid-afternoon slump. Each time you reach for that foil-wrapped bar, your brain builds receptors that make your body literally expect a treat every afternoon in order to feel satisfied. Each time you give in to the urge, the receptors become stronger. Before long, what you are experiencing isn't even a light desire; it's a full-on urge.

Resisting that urge takes real energy and determination, which is one reason many of our habits are so hard to break. That's particularly true where food and drink are concerned. The human body is an amazing machine that evolved to support a primitive hunter-gatherer lifestyle. Meals were sometimes few and far between, and the energy needed to live that kind of life was immense.

One way our species survived was by seeking out sugar and fat, which could sustain us through lean seasons. Those cravings, however, have not evolved to keep up with our modern lifestyle. Many of us, myself included, sit behind a computer all day and lead a relatively sedentary life. Consequently, our fat and sugar needs are significantly less than even those of our grandparents and great-grandparents.

For me, learning my body had been programmed over the millennia to crave something it no longer needs was a huge step. It taught me to recognize what's best for my 21st-century body in any given moment and motivated me to transform habits developed over years of acting upon cravings I misunderstood.

Many of us have developed emotional habits as well. These reactions are often based on our upbringing and previous experiences. If you were raised by quick-tempered parents who fought openly, you may be more likely to demonstrate anger. If rejection is a big trigger for you, you may push people away or, conversely, you may be particularly prone to latch on to someone, convinced you need them no matter how they treat you.

Regardless of what habits we've developed along our way, it is also true we all still have the ability to make a choice, to move from anger to joy and from self-doubt to self-love. Learning to do so is very much like building muscles in your body. In this case, it's about increasing your willpower to stop and be curious and to recognize how a habit might be informing your emotions and behavior.

The beneficial practice of pausing when triggered to assess what's actually happening can become a valuable habit of its own. All it requires is paying attention to your thoughts, the felt sensations in your body, and your emotions—and then choosing your next wise action based on your values.

Another way to outmaneuver the system is to replace a bad habit with a good habit. For instance, incorporating a healthy activity like taking an evening walk or adding a nighttime meditation session might be a great switch from a few cookies before going to bed. Not only will such activities support your mental and physical health in a sustainable way, but they will also become the kind of beneficial habits that change your life for the better.

As Cal State professor emeritus Loretta Graziano Breuning explains in her book *Habits of a Happy Brain*, we all seek out "feel-good" brain chemicals like dopamine and endorphins. Creating habits that encourage the release of these chemicals helps to reroute our brain's chemistry and foster more enjoyment in our lives.

Part of a mindfulness practice is teasing out which physical urges are habits and which are signals from our body indicating a real need or lack. For example, at fifty-eight years old, I'm well aware I've created more than a few habits when it comes to my food preferences, and not all of them are healthful.

My mindfulness practice helps me to ascertain which of those cravings are actually healthy for my body and which ones are no longer serving me. The only way to know for sure is to pay attention, to be curious, to make choices, and then to see what happens.

If we continue to learn as we go along, we can always apply that growing knowledge to future choices. The best way to know what is best for *your* mind, body, and spirit is to allow your life's daily experiences to be the stage where you implement exercises that encourage you to pay attention, be curious, and make choices. By learning from those choices again and again, you can actively apply your new-found knowledge to your future choices.

This is the key to living a life buoyed by an undercurrent of happiness. For instance, what happens if you opt to replace your afternoon chocolate with a cup of peppermint tea or some light stretching? Do you feel more alert? Do you feel better about your choices? How often do you actually miss or even crave the chocolate?

This I Believe: Or Do I?

Closely related to habits are our beliefs, or "the subconscious ideas that direct the way we see the world," as I define them. Because of how the human brain evolved and its great love of patterns, we are a species literally born to be great belief-makers.

As psychologist Michael Shermer explains in his wonderful book, *The Believing Brain: From Ghosts to Gods to Politics and Conspiracies—How We Construct Beliefs and Reinforce Them as Truths,* this propensity for making beliefs functions much like our love of sugar and fats when it comes to human survival over millennia.

Quickly associating the sound of heavy footsteps in tall grass with an approaching lion or tiger undoubtedly saved more than a few of our ancestors. It didn't matter how often that association proved true. The times they were wrong, all our forebears lost was a quick sprint to safety or a disrupted dinner or nighttime sleep. However, the consequences for *failing* to make that association were often deadly.

But just because these beliefs often served our early ancestors doesn't mean they necessarily continue to do so. As Shermer goes on to explain, our brains readily form beliefs without much—or even any—factual evidence to support them. And once our minds have latched onto a belief, it often tries to rationalize and support it, whether or not doing so is justified.

Consequently, we begin to use our beliefs as another prison house shade through which we view the world, choosing to see only those things that prove the legitimacy of the belief. Eventually, we don't even question its veracity—we just assume it's true and act accordingly.[2]

For many of us today, the basis of our beliefs comes from our culture, including the religion or spiritual practice in which we were raised. For instance, I mentioned in Chapter 1 that I came of age in the Catholic Church, where beliefs about an active and very present devil were common. The idea that we must always be on the lookout for evil defined my childhood in myriad ways.

As a young person, it kept me awake at night for fear that, once asleep, I could be caught unawares and ensnared by the devil. Church and parochial school only strengthened that belief until I was utterly convinced that the prospect of demonic possession lurked around every turn. I spent much of my childhood living largely in fear, often waking up in the middle of the night, frightened that the devil was coming for me.

As an adult, it took a lot of time, patience, courage, and daily mantras like "I am safe" and "I am protected" to undo the programming that belief had done.

If you've ever gone for a hike on a blazed trail, you know what the work of creating a new belief can look like. Blazes—those small painted rectangles, mostly on trees—are created by trail maintainers to mark a path.

A good trail crew will make sure that a blaze is always visible to hikers in either direction so they can find their way. Those blazes are required because what might look like an obvious trail in August will become completely covered in leaves by October.

No amount of human foot traffic is enough to create a visible path on rocky outcroppings or the sides of mountains, so the only way to designate the path is with those little painted rectangles. Sometimes, even those are hard to see.

Consequently, hikers often learn the hard way that staying on course requires focus, especially when it seems like there's a more direct or easier way to get where you're going. Creating new beliefs that are authentic to you and the way you want to live your life is like blazing and maintaining a trail in your mind. With each step you take, you are marking and reinforcing a pathway so the next time you find yourself in the same situation, the way forward will be made easier and more familiar.

What we gain from this practice is well worth the effort. Personally, I've come to really love and appreciate some of the new paths I've forged since adopting a mindful life. Here's one example that comes from my time behind the wheel.

The drive from my farmhouse into the small city where I work is awe-inspiring, no matter how many times I make it. The road itself is long and relatively untraveled, marked by undulating hills. On one side is a beautiful farm with its well-kept outbuildings, grain silos, picturesque hay fields, and a herd of contented black cows, each one wearing a unique yellow ear tag. In the spring, I often see calves dancing around in new clover.

In the fall, the fields become a vibrant gold and green, framed by crimson- and mustard-colored trees, which are perfectly complemented by the tidy white barn and outbuildings. Beyond those buildings, a line of trees frames the horizon, often capturing the sunlight in their leaves.

No matter the season, on days when I am being mindful, there is always something in this scene that grabs my attention, reminding me to pause for a moment of gratitude.

Summertime is a particularly beautiful season to make this drive. One recent summer morning, I was on my way to a meeting in the city. The sun was shining from behind me, illuminating the tips of the trees and creating the most breathtaking view.

However, instead of pausing to soak it all in, I was in my head, reviewing my obligations for the day. My typical "uniform" on most workdays is a black shirt paired with black slacks or a skirt. I don't know exactly where I got the idea, but I've always believed this color choice makes me look thinner (and truth be told, I welcome not having to color-coordinate clothes on a busy morning).

That particular morning, however, I'd made a bold choice: a blue skirt, white tank top, and a white wrap. I was running close to the wire for my first meeting, and I hadn't had time to eat breakfast at home. I hastily sliced an apple and tossed it on a plate, along with a heaping spoonful of peanut butter, and perched the plate on the passenger seat next to me. In between bites, I was sipping from a thermos filled with steaming hot coffee and trying to remind myself not to spill it on my white top.

Not long into the drive, I crested a steep hill, where the view was especially dramatic. As I did, I slowed my pace, paused my thinking, and allowed myself to be overwhelmed by the beauty of the scene. In my rapture, my car floated a bit left of center.

And just as it did, a car approached from the opposite direction. I quickly returned to my traveling lane and hit the brake, causing coffee to spill on my white shirt and wrap. As you might imagine, my initial reaction was a rush of frustration. I'd spent the better part of the drive reminding myself not to spill my coffee, and here I'd gone and done exactly that.

The jolt of the situation prompted me to slow down, and I continued on my way at far below my normal speed. A short time later, I navigated a sharp turn in the road, only to find a doe and her fawn standing right in the middle of the road. Had I been driving my habitual way, there's a good chance I would have hit them.

Instead, I easily tapped the brakes as they hopped off into a nearby cornfield. Immediately, I felt overwhelming relief and happiness: grateful I spilled my coffee and thankful the shame of almost causing an accident caused me to curtail my speed. I looked down at the coffee on my shirt and saw not so much an ugly stain as what looked like a perfect brown footprint. I couldn't help but smile.

In that moment, my willingness to be open to the unfolding scene rerouted what could have been a disastrous morning. In place of being angry or slipping into self-recrimination, I felt light and gratified knowing I had not only been witness to a particularly stunning pastoral scene but that my amended driving had saved the lives of two animals.

Rather than worrying about my schedule and whether or not I'd be on time, I found a different kind of meaning in the morning, and that meaning superseded any pre-existing habit or belief—and did indeed forge a new path for me. For the rest of that day, whenever I looked at the stain on my shirt, I chose to be thankful for what had created it.

Left to our own devices, many of us will allow unexamined habits and beliefs to dictate our relationships with ourselves, other people, and with the physical world around us. Mindfulness encourages us to pause and ask: *Is this true to who I am now? Is this who I want to be at this moment? Does this action or emotional attitude respect my values and the ways of being that are important to me?*

The answer to such questions brings unconscious thoughts and feelings into our consciousness through the process of interpreting ourselves. And once they are conscious, we can choose which thoughts to believe, which attitudes to discard or amplify, and ultimately, which actions to choose.

You have the ability to make all kinds of choices about how you live your life. Say, for instance, that over time, you have grown to believe you are terrible at meeting new people. Perhaps a disapproving parent scolded you for slouching in public or for speaking up at the dinner table. Maybe you were teased as a young child and began to withdraw. Perhaps a boss marginalized you for having a weak handshake or not generating spirited conversations with clients and guests.

You've since internalized that shame and now believe you're just awful in new social situations. Say, also, you just learned your company has announced a mandatory retreat for all of its satellite locations, and the thought of a weekend making pleasantries with strangers who also have sway over your career has you in a tailspin. You go home that night, beside yourself with anxiety, and immediately dig into a pint of triple chocolate ice cream, as is your habit whenever you're feeling stressed.

Typically, you might finish the entire pint with no awareness you're even eating it. But what if you rewound the scene to the moment you first walked up to the freezer? What if you paused there and quickly performed a body scan—feeling your feet on the floor, noting the thoughts in your head, emotions that might be present, and any physical sensations moving through your body?

Probably, you would discover a lot about what's happening inside your mind and body. Are you actually hungry, or are you looking to feed a psychological want or need? If your appearance at the freezer was a result of the latter, you could magnify the effects of the body scan by sharing with yourself an appreciation for how taxing the day felt and how capable you were at managing it.

Finally, to top off this mindful awareness and self-compassion, you could send yourself loving kindness and recite an affirmation like, "I am enough" or "I am doing my best job." Would you still want the ice cream? My guess is that if you did, a bite or two would satisfy you. The act of flicking that mental switch, of pausing to reflect and inviting yourself to change the narrative, creates and reinforces a new, more productive neural pathway.

Extra bonus: in turn, that new path will make it much easier to avoid the ice cream next time. Even better bonus: it may well create the mental space needed to question the belief that you are bad at social events and open up a new experience in which you begin to truly enjoy them.

The Little Green Guy Was Right: There Is No Try

If you're a *Star Wars* fan, you might remember the scenes in *The Empire Strikes Back* where Yoda teaches Luke Skywalker how to become a Jedi. At one particularly low moment, Luke begins to act like a petulant teenager when he finds he's unable to raise his X-wing fighter out of the swamp. He first pouts and, eventually, he gives up entirely.

You can tell by his adolescent mannerisms in this scene that Luke has entirely surrendered to self-doubt and the narratives of failure in his head. For his part, the Jedi Master is neither surprised nor persuaded. Instead, Yoda shakes his head with knowing bemusement, having already become accustomed to Luke's defeatist attitude.

"Always with you, it cannot be done," Yoda says. "You must unlearn what you have learned."

When the still decidedly defeatist Luke makes a half-hearted agreement to try again, Yoda stomps one of his tiny green feet.

"No," he insists. "Try not. Do. Or do not. There is no try."

And let me tell you: that diminutive sage was on to something really important.

As a life coach, I've learned to pay close attention to the power of the words we use and how they influence our thoughts and beliefs. Two of my least favorite words in the English language are also words I believe are significant roadblocks on the road to self-compassion: *should* and *try*.

The frenemies of unexamined beliefs, these seemingly simple words can set us up for a world of hurt and recrimination if we're not conscious of them. Whenever I hear a client use the words *should* or *try*, I have an inkling that the person, like Luke Skywalker, is relying on a long-standing habit or belief.

More to the point, I also have a sneaking suspicion that that habit or belief comes from an expectation that either my client's family, social circle, or peer group has set, rather than an ideal my client has accepted for themselves.

Trigger words like "should" or "try" often indicate we've been confronted with an imposed commitment or responsibility that doesn't align with our own values. Instead, they've been thrust upon us, most likely by family, authority figures, or past friends.

Some textbook examples of how we tend to use these words include:

- I *should* wear heels to the party tonight.
- I'll *try* to get to church on Sunday.
- I *should* get these holiday cards out before the new year.
- I'll *try* to find time to exercise this weekend.

All of those statements are a clear indication to me that the people uttering them are driven by a belief about the expectations others have for them rather than what they want for themselves. Often, we use words like "should" and "try" because we don't want to disappoint or hurt other people.

We believe we *should* visit a difficult relative because we've been told it's the good or decorous thing to do—that we have a duty to do so, rather than because we've consciously decided it's the best thing for us at any given moment. We accept these ideas as beliefs and rarely stop to interrogate or revise them.

Along the way, we begin to cajole ourselves with internal dialogue about how we should dress or what our social obligations are, rather than pausing to ask ourselves what is important to us and will bring us satisfaction and joy.

Each time I become aware I am using words like *should* or *try*, I hear the tinkle of a little bell in my mind, inviting me to be curious about any unconscious beliefs that may be impacting my thinking and potentially influencing my next action. I ask myself why I feel obligated to do something (in the case of a *should*) or what's preventing me from fully committing (in the case of a *try*).

Oftentimes, simply pausing to ask those questions is enough to create a powerful emotional response. That response can raise awareness in me about possible resentments, assumptions, or expectations I feel or have. It illuminates roadblocks I've been experiencing that have prevented me from embracing a task, and it raises my awareness that I'm giving in to what feels like an obligation rather than an opportunity. It also demonstrates where I've chosen to adopt societal expectations rather than choosing what's best (and, in the case of the high heels, *most comfortable*) for me.

Most of us have adopted some of society's expectations, cultural beliefs, and assumed habits. And that's understandable, given how our species has evolved. Ours is a communal, social species. We survived for thousands of years abiding by the expectations of our tribe, and excommunication from that tribe was tantamount to death.

Today, the power of what society expects of us continues to play a significant role for us, even though we aren't dependent on our tribesmen and women to keep us safe from starvation and the threat of giant predators. We remain programmed to think collectively and make choices we hope will please others. We hate to say no for fear we might displease or disappoint another member of our community. That's all well and good, so long as those choices are conscious and don't fly in the face of our personal values or even our health.

We'll talk more in Chapter 6 about values and how they relate to the mindfulness journey, but for now, it's enough to say that in this context, I define values as "principles or standards that reflect what is important to us."

However, before we get to that next chapter, let's go back to this idea of forging a trail through the woods. With or without the tree blazes, our brains establish paths in much the same way. Remarkable advances in the field of neuroscience have mapped how brains think, create habits, and build beliefs.

We know now that every time certain brain cells communicate, they forge a connection that strengthens with each subsequent communication. This is known as neuroplasticity, and it allows our brains to form and strengthen pathways for specific behaviors, thoughts, and emotions.

Eventually, these pathways become so ingrained they become automatic behaviors that allow us to ride a bike or button a shirt without consciously thinking about how to do either. Instead, it becomes rote—an almost mechanical response that doesn't require the heavy exertion of thinking about each step.

However, when we flip the switch to making mindful choices about even the most mundane exercise, we also build our greater capacity for neuroplasticity and growth. Each time we choose to make that choice, we are promoting greater neuroplasticity by encouraging repeated attention to specific sensations, thoughts, or emotions, thus strengthening the connections between the neurons involved in those experiences.

One of the leaders in this field is Rick Hanson, a psychologist, senior fellow at the University of California-Berkeley's Greater Good Science Center, and a *New York Times* best-selling author. His research has demonstrated the way our brains privilege mindful thinking as they grow and change. Specifically, our neurons become more active when they are presented with information that arrives as a result of focused attention.

Just like the prospect of being eaten by a tiger made our ancestors more alert, mindfully focusing on what thoughts we're thinking helps to solidify them and build stronger pathways. In other words, every moment we take for mindfulness, we are encouraging what Hanson calls "beneficial brain change": we become more aware, more loving, and more resilient. In sum, we become a better, more realized version of ourselves.[3]

Given the stakes involved, it's reasonable to wonder whether or not you are on the right path. One way to identify how you are doing in building this better self is by noticing your emotions as they arise.

Another approach is to be aware of when you use words like "should" or "try." Let those words act as a gentle alarm to notify you that more awareness is required. Take a moment to pause and notice felt sensations in your body and the emotional states they represent.

If you identify strong emotions like anger, invite yourself to be curious. Ask yourself, *How does anger manifest in my body? Where am I feeling it right now? What does it look like? Sound like? What thoughts might be influencing my emotions and feelings and vice-versa?*

Begin to take stock of how emotions manifest in your body and what result the emotions and physical sensations have on your thoughts and ideas. Learn to recognize who you are—and who you become—in those moments.

Speaking personally, I have identified two personas who love to rear their ugly heads when challenging emotions come into play. I like to call the first of these personalities "Little Miss Perfect." I've learned to recognize when she appears on the stage because I tend to feel manic—like my entire body is vibrating.

When Little Miss Perfect appears, I can no longer sit still. My thoughts are erratic like I've had *way* too much caffeine. Over time, I've come to understand that Little Miss Perfect tends to arrive when I have too much on my plate, or my life is feeling out of control. She's great at reminding me I've overscheduled myself or, if I've missed a crucial deadline or detail, I'm worthless. If I'm hosting an important event, you can be sure Little Miss Perfect will appear to question my catering choices, guest list, or whether people like me enough to show up.

I refer lovingly to the second persona as "Crazy Bitch." You got a brief glimpse of her at the start of this chapter when I described some of my least proud driving moments. Crazy Bitch is definitely not someone you want to answer to in a meeting. She's unpredictable, reactive, and quick to show disapproval when things don't play out as planned. She can be highly aggressive, and worst of all, she's a total know-it-all. Crazy Bitch is also disappointingly self-serving, not open to feedback, and demands everything go her way. I know when she's around because my jaw becomes clenched, my shoulders rise up to my ears, my chest tightens, and I feel like I'm ready for a fight.

It's taken years of mindfulness practice for me to learn how best to close the door on Little Miss Perfect and Crazy Bitch. My mindfulness journey has taught me valuable skills about ways in which to identify their imminent arrival, what their arrival signifies, and the choices I need to make to send them packing.

Some of those techniques include a quick five-minute meditation sit or breathing techniques like those at the end of this chapter. But often, the most effective tool for escorting them off the stage is simply noticing they've arrived in the first place.

Chapter 5 Takeaways

- Thoughts and feelings can arise out of nowhere and do not necessarily reflect our true nature. They are the result of chemical and autonomic responses in our brains. As Jack Kornfield puts it, "Thoughts think themselves."

- Understanding the chemical reality of our thoughts and feelings can help us create useful distance from them. Once we understand we are not our thoughts, we can allow them to come and go without judgment or without embodying what they represent. Doing so creates greater self-compassion, too.

- A valuable exercise when faced with a negative thought or emotion is to pause and ask if it's true. For instance, if we are confronted with a thought like, "I'm a failure," we can pause to examine that idea and reflect on all of the instances in which we have disproven it through our words and deeds.

- An important part of any mindfulness journey is recognizing that part of being human involves making mistakes and not always acting like our best selves. We can use these moments to develop compassion and forgiveness.

- A habit is any action (including mental processes or thoughts) you perform so often you no longer need to be mindful or conscious when performing it.

- Habits can be difficult to break because, each time we perform them, we strengthen connections in our brains, including some that have evolved over millennia to keep our species alive.

- One way to break a bad habit is to replace it with a good one. For example, we can reach for a cup of herbal tea or a piece of fruit whenever we crave ice cream or chocolate.

- Beliefs are subconscious ideas that direct the way we see the world. Over generations, our brains evolved to create beliefs intended to keep us safe, which also means they tend to focus upon (and often exaggerate) perceived threats, even if there isn't evidence to support them.

- For many of us, our beliefs are first instilled and then reinforced through our cultures: our religious affiliation, our ethnicity or community of origin, and our families—both assigned and chosen.

- Mindfulness encourages us to examine our beliefs. By pausing to reflect upon them, we move our beliefs from the sub- or unconscious and create a space where we can make a conscious choice to accept, discard, challenge, or revise our beliefs before they dictate our behavior.

- Be on the lookout for trigger words like "should" and "try." These qualifiers are often evidence that a decision has been made based on unexamined beliefs and may well be incongruous with our goals and best versions of ourselves.

- By questioning our habits and beliefs, we build greater neuroplasticity and create additional connections and pathways in the brain.

Chapter 5 Exercises

Formal Mindfulness Practice

Yoga Postures to Raise Your Spirit and Improve Your Mood

Taking a few moments to practice yoga postures can be an excellent way to increase circulation and oxygen levels; they can also relieve stress and quiet the nervous system. These three poses work to do both. If you are new to yoga, consider consulting a physician or certified yoga instructor to ensure this practice is safe and performed correctly. And remember: although some yoga poses can stretch our muscles or test our core strength, they should never feel painful or create sharp sensations. If you experience either, safely exit the pose.

MOUNTAIN POSE (Tadasana)

This foundational practice, Mountain Pose, invites you to cultivate a sense of groundedness and stability. It is designed to help you develop mindful awareness of your body's alignment and balance. By practicing this pose, you may find yourself standing with greater confidence, experiencing a deeper connection to the earth, and fostering a calm, centered state of mind.

Begin by finding a stable, quiet place where you can practice without interruption. Stand tall with your feet hip-width apart, allowing your weight to be evenly distributed across both feet. Notice the sensations in your feet as they make contact with the ground.

You might also imagine roots extending from your soles deep into the earth, grounding and supporting you (I often pivot on my feet gently in a circle, moving the weight of my body around my foot until I feel a balanced distribution of pressure and body weight). Allow your toes to spread gently, creating a firm foundation.

As you inhale, softly lengthen your spine, lifting through the crown of your head. Roll your shoulders back and down. Let your shoulders relax. Allow your arms to hang naturally by your sides, palms facing forward.

Take a moment to scan your body, noticing any areas of tension or tightness. Without judgment, allow these areas to soften with each breath. As you stand in Mountain Pose, observe the subtle shifts and changes in your body's balance.

Continue to allow yourself to simply be in this pose, fully present with your body and breath. When you're ready, gently release the pose by bringing your awareness back to the room around you.

DOWNWARD FACING DOG (Adho Mukha Svanasana)

Downward Facing Dog invites you to stretch and lengthen your body, creating space and openness in your spine and hamstrings. This practice encourages mindful attention to the sensations in your body, promoting both strength and relaxation.

Begin in a tabletop position, with your hands directly under your shoulders and your knees under your hips. Spread your fingers wide, grounding through your palms. Take a deep breath in. As you exhale, lift your knees off the floor, and slowly begin to straighten your legs, bringing your hips up towards the sky.

Pause and notice the sensations in your body. Notice the thoughts and judgments that move through your mind.

If you are able, gently reach your heels to the ground without forcing them to touch. Allow your head to hang naturally between your arms, releasing any tension in your neck. With each inhale, imagine creating more space along your spine, and with each exhale, gently deepen into the pose.

As you hold this pose, observe the sensations in your body—the stretch, the strength, the balance. If your mind begins to wander, gently bring it back to the rhythm of your breath. When you're ready, slowly lower your knees back to the floor, returning to the tabletop position.

COBRA POSE (Bhujangasana)

Cobra Pose is a practice of gentle back bending that invites you to open your heart and chest while strengthening your back. This pose is a heart opener. It encourages a mindful exploration of your body's capacity for openness and resilience.

Begin by lying face down on your mat, with your legs extended behind you and the tops of your feet resting on the ground. Place your hands under your shoulders, fingers spread wide. Allow your elbows to tuck in close to your body.

As you inhale, gently press into your palms, slowly lifting your chest off the ground. Keep your elbows slightly bent and close to your sides so your lower ribs stay connected to the floor. Allow your mind's eye to travel the length of your chest, back, and spine, noticing physical sensations, emotions, and thoughts.

Relax your shoulders away from your ears, creating space in your neck. Keep your gaze soft, looking slightly forward or down, and breathe deeply into the stretch. With each inhale, subtly expand your chest, and with each exhale, release any tension in your back or shoulders.

If your mind wanders, gently guide it back to your breath. When you're ready, slowly lower your chest back to the ground, resting your forehead on the mat and allowing your body to relax completely.

Take a moment to notice how your body feels after the pose, appreciating the effort and care you've given yourself.

Informal Mindfulness Practice

Exercise in Letting Go

If I'm paying attention, I find I have a litany of judgments about what's happening in any given moment: I'm too cold or too hot, I've been sitting too long, or I ate too much. Possibly, I didn't eat at all or failed to drink enough water. I'll notice my coffee table is cluttered, my sofa needs to be cleaned, or my windows need to be washed.

These all seem like silly annoyances, and yet they clutter up my brain. If left completely unchecked, this mounting collection of little things can become an underlying anxiety that affects my entire state of mind.

Exercises in letting go strengthen your self-awareness and foster curiosity. There's nothing to add to your calendar here. The practice is to simply notice what's happening during an ordinary activity you perform habitually.

To begin, start by setting alarms at random times throughout your day to remind you to pause and pay attention. Do this using whatever method and in any way feels right for you (I personally like to use the calendar on my Smartphone).

When your alarm or chime sounds, pause for a moment, take a gentle breath in and out, and move your attention inward to check in with your body. Allow yourself to simply be present to your physical sensations.

What do you notice? When you check in with your thoughts, what judgments are present? Are you thinking about the past or the future? Look around you; what do you notice? Do the sensations in your body shift as you observe your world? What thoughts are present?

Finally, ask yourself the question, "What can I let go of here?" Then, notice if a thought comes into your mind.

The simple act of inviting yourself to let go will shift your physical sensations. Often, I'm not aware of a judgment that's being released, and yet my shoulders drop, or the muscles of my neck soften.

Take one last conscious breath in and out, and send gratitude to yourself and all the things that align in order for you to be present in this moment.

••• 6 •••

Not Good or Bad, But Curious

ONE OF THE first challenges I had to overcome along my mindfulness path was abandoning my black-and-white ideas. I was still so conditioned to believe in the two mutually exclusive categories of *good* and *bad* that my first foray into mindfulness was completely defined by those beliefs.

The conversations inside my head during those early days were all about whether I was being a good or bad meditator and whether I was practicing the right or wrong way. That habit of judging my behaviors and thoughts has been a very hard one to break, and I still catch myself in this cycle of judgments.

However, the more I began to practice mindfulness, the more awareness I began to gain about how, when, and why I slipped into those kinds of reductive judgments. This kind of awareness is one of the first and greatest gifts a mindfulness practice offers.

Once we become aware of our habituated judgments and behaviors, we have the opportunity to choose whether or not we want to continue in these thoughts and actions. We give ourselves the freedom and ability to make choices when we let ourselves become curious about our judgments rather than just embracing them as true or condemning ourselves for having thought them in the first place.

Mindfulness encourages us to be curious and to explore those judgments and reactions with thoughtfulness and much self-compassion. Along the way, our old narratives begin to change from "I can't believe I was so stupid" to something like, "The story my brain is telling me is that I'm bad. I wonder why?"

Once we begin to forgo these old, judgy narratives and replace them with loving self-examination, we can learn a lot about not only our true selves but who we want to be in the world. The more we understand about our values and principles, the more we can make conscious choices that allow us to embody our best selves.

That not only leads to greater self-respect and self-esteem, it also has the power to radically transform our relationships with others as well, from our loved ones to our employees and supervisors. And as these relationships improve and transform, you'll have more time and energy to dedicate to the goals and people that matter most.

The Roots of Our Feelings

One of my favorite movies is *Under the Tuscan Sun*. In it, the main character, Frances, played by Diane Lane, is a successful writer who learns that her unemployed husband is having an affair. As part of the divorce arrangements, she agrees to cede her half of their house to him and his (much younger) new girlfriend.

Frances then moves into a miserable apartment, where she soon finds she's too depressed to write. Instead, she begins to wallow in her sad and bitter feelings until her best friend Patti, played by Sandra Oh, becomes understandably concerned.

Patti has just learned she's pregnant, so she offers Frances her place on an Italian tour: *You're at a crossroads in your life*, says Patti (I'm paraphrasing here). *You can either put on your big girl pants, get out of this funk, and move on with your life, or you can become an embittered old lady who lives with ten cats.*

Happily, Lane's character chooses the former. On the Italian tour, she spies an advertisement for a decrepit villa and decides to reinvent herself by renovating it. I won't give away the ending but suffice to say it's a happy one.

So much of our lives can be boiled down to the assertion made by Sandra Oh's character: when faced with a difficult or painful situation, we can make the choice to wallow, or we can choose happiness.

Yes, experiences like divorce or loss come with undeniably powerful and complex emotions; yes, we need to acknowledge and progress through those emotional states if we are to heal. However, it's also important to recognize that our brains can become accustomed to those uncomfortable states, even if they fail to serve us.[1]

Without even consciously intending to, we can habituate ourselves to experiencing emotions like sorrow, thereby teaching our minds to seek out experiences that will foster those emotions.

Although we don't become addicted to emotions in the same way we become addicted to substances or behaviors, our brains do develop patterns and cravings for emotional experiences, even if we know they lead to more discomfort and unhappiness. That is in part because, when faced with either internal or external stimuli, the nervous system actually reorganizes its structures and connections.

One way this occurs is through the release of neurotransmitters, chemical messengers that send signals between cells. Dopamine, for instance, is a particularly powerful example of these hormones, and its effects create the sensation of pleasure.

Once we've experienced a dopamine rush, we begin to seek it out wherever we can. Eventually, our cells begin to crave that hormone just to feel normal. This can occur in obvious ways, such as an addiction to nicotine or opiates. However, our bodies have other sources for feel-good hormones like dopamine, including exercise, meditation, or even sex.

The more we experience the feel-good sensations associated with these activities, the more our brain begins to seek out that experience.

The same is true for other chemical responses as well. Consider the sympathetic nervous system, which puts us in the fight-flight-freeze state. As we've seen in previous chapters, this system releases powerful hormones that heighten our awareness and perception of danger.

People who experience a significant amount of stress in their lives will eventually become habituated to the sensations those hormones produce and may even seek out stressful experiences to simply feel normal. The good news is we can use mindfulness to enhance our brain's ability to favor pleasure and happiness.

But how do we know when we're experiencing real joy versus just the momentary conditioned response to, say, online shopping or a box of Girl Scout cookies? Simple: We begin with a thorough inventory of our values and what matters most to us. It's only through this personal reflection that we can learn what happiness and fulfillment really looks like to each of us.

One of my roles as a life coach and mindfulness instructor is to help my clients engage in this kind of reflection and to support the learning and growth that results in making more fulfilling choices.

When I teach workshops, for instance, I'll often begin by asking participants to set agreements for themselves. This is an opportunity for them to reflect upon what it is they really want out of the experience—along with ways the group can support their sense of safety and how I and the other participants can support them in meeting their goals or intentions for attending the workshop.

This exercise also serves the very valuable function of encouraging participants to identify and articulate their needs. Too often, we don't ask for what we want, either because we don't know what we want or because we feel like it's not our place to do so. We've been taught that speaking up for ourselves is a sign of greed or selfishness rather than self-advocacy and realization. One of the most important things we can do on our mindfulness journeys is to pause and take time to choose what will be best for our personal health and well-being.

Valuing Values

From the moment we're born, our minds begin working overtime, processing sensory information, memories, and ideas. Even as young children, we're taught to prioritize some ideas over others. Ideally, this teaches us the importance of equanimity, kindness, and generosity.

However, it can also teach us to form and maintain biases and prejudices, particularly where social groups are concerned. Regardless of their origins or specific nature, these attitudes and principals are what also form the basis of our values. Over the years, we accumulate values from our family, our religious organizations, the cultural affiliations we maintain, and our lived experiences.

All of these values are then stored in our memory banks or subconscious brains. We may think they lie there dormant or that they've been expunged completely, but often, they're just quietly kicking around in there, masquerading as new thoughts or ideas.

Part of being mindful includes making conscious choices about which values we want to maintain because they reflect our ethics and beliefs and which ones we want to discard either because they don't serve us or because they are merely the result of our social conditioning. Especially initially, making this determination can feel hard.

One way to begin is to return to Byron Katie and her prompts for self-examination. You'll recall in Chapter 5 that I introduced two questions Katie encourages people to ask of themselves: "Is This True?" and "How do I know it's true?" To really focus on your values, consider a third question: "Does this align with my values?"

Let me explain how this works by way of my own journey. I said earlier that my early embrace of mindfulness came with the recognition that my brain thinks a surprising number of judgy or critical thoughts. Without even realizing it, I might have a derogatory response to what someone is wearing, what they said, or even what kind of car they're driving.

Say I walk into a grocery store to pick up a loaf of bread. At the checkout lane, the woman in front of me is wearing a pair of wrinkled pajama bottoms, a revealing tank top, and a pair of furry house slippers. My judgmental mind might think something like, *Wow, you really go shopping in your pajamas? I wouldn't be caught dead wearing that!* Those thoughts might then lead me in all kinds of unhelpful directions, like thinking additional demeaning thoughts about that woman or creating reproachful stories about myself because I thought critically about the woman in the first place.

Consider, on the other hand, what would happen if I paused long enough to ask myself: *Does judging this woman for her attire align with my values?* In this particular case, that's an easy question for me to answer. Some of my most ardently held values include compassion and tolerance, grace and kindness, positivity, and understanding.

The mere act of reminding myself about these values helps those negative thoughts about my fellow shopper float away. It also reminds me I don't know her story, and the realization that I don't know what struggles she's experiencing quickly reroutes my brain to a more empathetic connection to our shared humanness.

Reminding myself of my values quiets down the judgy voice in my head and replaces those ideas with feelings of connection and compassion.

Many of our thoughts and choices seem to stem from our unconscious brain. Merely recognizing that fact can be the motivation to bring them to the foreground in our conscious mind. Making a commitment to examine our thoughts allows us to identify the pre-existing ideas and biases that influence our decision-making.

Mindfulness helps us to notice and examine how thoughts influence the ways we see and experience the world; it also reminds us of the power of the metaphoric pause button. By taking a deep, intentional breath or noticing the feeling of our feet on the floor, we create a space between our thoughts and beliefs and the ways we may choose to act upon them.

This space can provide the opportunity to ask whether those thoughts align with our values and to decide whether we will choose to respond to those thoughts in a way that promotes our best selves.

We tend to give our brains a lot of power and autonomy. If a thought appears, we're inclined to accept it without much examination. But the fact of the matter is we can all choose which thoughts we want to believe or encourage. We can also ask ourselves which of those thoughts are actually true. That, in turn, allows us to explore the ways in which our values affect our choices and contribute to our overall sense of well-being.

It's important to note when I use the word "value," I'm not referring to the idea of morals and ethics, which I define as a code of conduct established by a social group. Values are those individually held beliefs and principles that dictate our behavior. As such, they are unique to individuals.

In some cases, values might be traits or systems we're born with—a tendency toward humor and play, cleanliness and orderliness, or the need to spend time alone. Values can also be learned or influenced by our families and other close social cohorts. If you are raised in a religious community, values such as modesty and faith may be particularly important to you.

Regardless from whence they come, values are neither good nor bad, nor are they necessarily shared by your partner or close friends. They're best thought of as "ways of being," which is to say they are ways of living your life that are particularly important to you.

When it comes to identifying your own values, consider beginning with this question: "What are some of the attitudes and characteristics that are most important to me?"

These might include concepts like freedom and independence, respect and family, honesty, and justice.

Another way of thinking about values is as the list of character traits you embody when you feel the most alive and are living as your best self. To generate that list, ask yourself: "What's happening inside and around me when I feel like my most authentic self and the most comfortable in my own skin?"

Perhaps you feel your best when you grab a sketch pad and begin drawing or spend an hour at a potter's wheel. If so, creativity may be a value of yours. Perhaps it's the knowledge that you finished a difficult task at work, which might signal values such as productivity, accountability, or resilience.

Say you're someone for whom workouts are non-negotiable. No matter the season or what else is going on in your life, you always find the time to hit the gym. Most likely, there's a powerful value underlying that choice. It could be determination or hard work, health or vitality. Then again, maybe it's fitness for its own sake.

In any case, taking the time to examine that motivation can tell you a lot about who you are and what you hold dear. It also goes a long way toward ensuring your choices are conscious rather than habits or addictions.

An effective way to discover your core values is to develop a regular practice of journal writing. Take the time to reflect upon your response to situations. Be curious. What qualities or ways of being did a particular experience bring out in you? Which of those qualities disappointed you? Which ones made you feel proud?

It can also be helpful to reflect upon those questions as they apply to others. Say you had an interaction with your supervisor at work. Were there behaviors in your boss you particularly admired? Or was there something he or she said or a behavior that disappointed, hurt, or angered you?

Practice identifying the emotion you experienced. Then ask yourself: *What was it about that action that brought me joy or caused me pain? What does that say about what's important to me?* You might also take the time to reflect upon the people and situations that most inspire and bring you joy. What qualities do you most appreciate in those individuals? In what circumstances do you feel happiest and most at ease? Is it when you are surrounded by family? Taking a solitary hike? Making cookies for someone you love or fighting for justice?

Remember: There are no right or wrong answers. The important thing is you identify that which you hold dear.

The more we participate in this kind of personal inquiry, the easier it becomes to recognize patterns—to notice the values that consistently rise to the surface, the situations that either reinforce or compromise those values, and the thoughts, emotions, and physical sensations you experience in those situations.

Say you have a supervisor who demands a lot of overtime work. You may begin to feel resentful of your job or victimized by your supervisor. If, in those circumstances, you were to take the time to sit down and reflect upon the situation and its relationship to your values, you may find insights that allow you to choose greater happiness in the long run. This could include being curious about why it's important to please your boss.

Is it because you want a promotion or a higher salary? Is it because you dislike conflict or want to avoid disappointing someone? On the other hand, if you're feeling resentful or powerless, can you get to the bottom of what's making you feel that way?

Perhaps it's because you yearn for a more active role in the lives of your kids or more time for hobbies. Or maybe because you value self-respect and autonomy over a paycheck.

Figuring out the "why" in these situations can reveal important things about who we are and how we want to live our lives.

These kinds of personal reflections take time. One of the things that's particularly challenging about identifying values is they can't always be distilled down to a single word. For instance, I really detest gossip. Honoring another person's authentic experience is very important to me, and when someone gossips about another person's story, they're really just filtering it through their own assumptions and expectations.

Gossip, to me, comes with an inherent dishonesty and lack of respect. That said, what does this aversion say about my values? For starters, it demonstrates the emphasis I place on honoring all people's authentic experience. It also reveals my commitment to not making assumptions or having expectations about myself or others and to finally being impeccable with my word.[2]

Put that way, all three of these statements are also statements of value:

1. I value the experience of others.

2. I value keeping an open, judgment-free mind.

3. I value being honest and trustworthy.

One way I know when I'm not living my values is by the way a particular situation feels in my body. For instance, whenever I hear someone gossiping, I get a bad feeling—an icky sensation in the pit of my stomach. Perhaps you feel anger when you see an animal mistreated; perhaps the prospect of a confrontation makes you feel nauseated or fearful.

In each of these situations, your body may be alerting you to the fact that your values have been compromised or offended. Our bodies often respond when we act in a way that offends our values. By being more aware of those physical reactions, we can also gain important insight about the values prompting those reactions. For me, personally, the experience of a lead weight in the pit of my stomach is a good indication I'm not abiding by one or more of my values.

Knowing my values helps me make confident decisions about my actions and choices that ensure I act in a way that is authentic to my best self. For example, I can choose not to spread gossip nor to listen when it is being spoken by others. Similarly, even though I'm awful at sending thank-you notes, I know it's the right thing to do. When I do manage to send a thank-you note, I feel a tremendous sense of accomplishment.

Why?

Because I value the act of acknowledging people and letting them know how much I appreciate them. Even though I dread the act of writing the notes, I'm proud of myself when they're finished because I've had the opportunity to send words of affirmation to someone I care about and to strengthen the connection we have.

Whenever we have a strong emotional reaction like joy or anger, there is likely a core value motivating the emotion. For instance, it took my explosion at that Labor Day clambake for me to understand just how often I allow people to break the boundaries I set and how often I turn a blind eye both to my own values and the feelings they produce. Sometimes, those feelings are complex and even seemingly at odds with one another. That's because we all have a list of values, and they are not always in concert with one another.

Take my tendency toward aggressive driving: I get riled up by slow drivers because they are compromising my freedom (a very important value to me); I also get riled up by being riled up because peacefulness is another important value of mine. So, while I love to be behind the wheel of a car as an exercise of personal freedom, I also recognize that doing so may compromise my desire for peace.

In that case, I have to choose which of my values is the most important to me.

Whenever people tell me they feel like they don't have a choice in a particular situation or they blame someone or something else for their current experience, that's usually a signal to me that they have competing values at play. If those individuals can isolate those values, assess the importance of each of them, and make an intentional decision about which principle, characteristic, or state of mind happens to be most important in the moment, they often find the choice is actually quite clear.

Take the example of having a supervisor who demands long overtime hours. You may feel like you have no choice but to stay in the job. However, if you really examine what's going on, it could be that your desire to provide a financially stable life for your family is competing with your desire to spend time with your family.

Or perhaps your desire for career advancement is competing with your desire for health or travel. If you decide that what you really value is financial stability and routine, you may choose to stay in your job and relinquish the resentment and feelings of victimization. Better yet, you may set boundaries around that job and your interactions with your supervisor.

If you decide that time with your family or a schedule that allows you to join an adult soccer league is of a higher value, that may be the motivation needed to begin a search for a new job. Then again, you may feel like financial security is most important to you—at least until your kids graduate from college. In that case, choosing to stay in your job may feel best to you.

In either of these situations, you'll at least have the satisfaction of knowing you are choosing consciously and with a greater sense of empowerment.

When we allow ourselves to be curious about our values, we can discover the memories, perceptions, biases, and prejudices that lurk in our subconscious and influence our responses to people and situations. I like to think of this practice as another example of a metaphorical mindfulness gym workout: we're building muscles and the strength that comes with them.

Just as a good bodybuilder knows to work on both biceps *and* triceps, mindfulness requires us to work on different mental muscles as well. When it comes to values, we can make a conscious choice to develop certain character traits that create a sense of balance and wholeness in our lives. Choosing to focus on values that promote that sense of well-being is another important step toward choosing to live a happy and joy-filled life.

Spelunking for Values

How do we best begin to identify our values? Vulnerability researcher and best-selling author Brené Brown has created a list of more than one hundred commonly held values. The table below includes some of those values, including:

Ambition	Freedom	Resourcefulness
Authenticity	Fun	Self-Expression
Belonging	Generosity	Spirituality
Career	Growth	Time
Compassion	Health	Tradition
Creativity	Humor	Truth

Curiosity	Loyalty	Understanding
Dignity	Nature	Vision
Family	Order	Vulnerability
Financial Stability	Power	Wisdom

To identify some of your values, take a few moments to study this partial list. Are there certain words that jump out to you? You may also simply reflect on each of the words and notice your thoughts, emotions, and physical sensations as you do so.

Do any of these words bring up a story, an emotion, or any discernible physical sensations? How does the experience of meditating on a particular word feel in your body? Is there someone you particularly admire who embodies that value? Take the time to note these responses in a diary or journal. If you don't notice any responses, that's okay, too; you may choose to reflect on this list at a later date and discover that your reactions have changed.

In my experience, the strength of the emotional response individuals have to a word on this list is directly proportional to the importance of that particular value in their lives. Knowing the importance of a value can be helpful in deciding when and if to compromise that value.

Similarly, the severity of any negative emotional experience that occurs if and when you compromise a core value can say a lot about that value's importance in your life. If you notice a particularly sharp or intense emotional experience, you may want to catalog it in your journal. In the same way, if a word elicits no emotion from you, simply make a note of that, too.

And remember: the above list is a very incomplete one. There are almost as many values as there are people who hold them. Just because a word on this particular list doesn't resonate with you doesn't mean you lack concrete values. Consider this list (and these exercises) as a starting point and an opportunity to practice noticing and naming your core values.

That experience can be further enhanced by taking time each day to notice what activities make you feel particularly happy and joyful or even those that leave you feeling angry, frustrated, or apathetic. It can also be useful to observe activities that spark action toward change and those that leave you feeling trapped or helpless.

To bring this kind of inquiry into your daily life, begin by creating a list of which activities regularly evoke a pleasant or unpleasant emotion in you. Next to each activity, identify the emotion the activity evokes. For instance, you may find yourself writing "bird watching" and "peacefulness" or "cooking" and "love."

After you have identified these activities, select one and return to your list of values. For those activities that spark pleasant emotions, see if you can pair them with specific values on your list. For those that lead to unpleasant emotional experiences, ask yourself which, if any, of your values that activity disrespects or undermines.

Permission to Drive the Bus

Before I realized the importance of understanding and living by my values, I spent a lot of time doing things I didn't really want to do. I'd find myself agreeing to serve on committees or spending a day engaged in an activity that either I had no interest in, or that didn't utilize my strengths and unique abilities.

I often felt victimized by the choices and decisions I was making, even though I was the one making them. I felt I was living by other people's rules, behaving in ways, and agreeing to things I believed would encourage people to like me or make them feel happy.

When I finally woke up to the fact that I was in the driver's seat of my life—that everything I did and all the ways I spent my time were the results of choices I had made, I set the intention to become more conscious of my choices. I also committed to embodying these values and to living by their guidelines every day.

In practice, setting the intention to embody and live by a set of values also involves setting boundaries—first with yourself, then with everyone around you. By definition, a boundary is a clear demarcation line that defines the limits of an area. It's the act of communicating your expectations, asking for what you want, and clearly saying "no" to things you don't want.

There are three aspects to setting a strong boundary, what I call the "Three C's of Boundary Setting": *clarify, communicate,* and *commit.*

1. **Clarify the *what* and the *why* of your boundaries.** What are the values you want to respect? Be clear about the importance of each value in your life. How will living by these values keep you healthy, happy, fulfilled, and purposeful? How do the people around you benefit by respecting your values? If two values are in conflict, which will you privilege and why?

2. **Communicate your boundaries clearly and compassionately.** When communicating these values with loved ones or colleagues, show respect for their concerns and wishes by listening openly and without judgment. Work out in advance what, if any, part of your value you are willing to compromise and for what reasons.

3. **Commit to upholding your boundaries.** Practice the words you will use to reiterate your boundaries and be prepared to explain over and over again the *what* and the *why* of your boundaries.

Too often, we decide it's easier to suffer through something rather than asking for what we really want. Many of us were taught that articulating our wants and needs makes us seem greedy; we learned that saying "no" or establishing boundaries is a sign of selfishness.

In reality, setting clear and healthy boundaries is one of the best things we can do for a relationship. When we set boundaries, we are clearly articulating what we need from the relationship in order to feel happy, fulfilled, appreciated, and respected. We are modeling self-respect and self-care and opening a dialogue that invites others to do the same.

Initially, I was really lousy at this kind of boundary setting. I never wanted to upset people or appear as if I thought my needs were more important than theirs. At times, it felt like the commitments I made had me at war with myself. I was clumsy, my experiences were fraught with tears and frustration, and I was very uncomfortable.

In the case of that infamous clambake at our lake house, for instance, I knew asking people to sleep outside and to keep their pets at home was a way for all of us to have a good time. I could be a happy and gracious host, knowing the chaos of clutter and people would end when the day was over. Dogs left at home would be safe from cars traveling along the road; children closely monitored would be safe as well; and children staying outdoors, unless accompanied by at least one parent, would help me feel respected as the host.

The problem was I didn't clarify those boundaries with myself, my husband, or the guests at the beginning of the party. Throughout the day, I felt myself getting more and more agitated. And somewhere along the way, I was eventually reminded of the story of the boiling frog.

As the story goes, if a frog is tossed into boiling water, it will quickly hop out, saving itself from certain harm. If, on the other hand, that frog is first placed into slightly warm water, the frog will stay there, not realizing the danger it's in. Eventually, as the temperature increases in nearly imperceptible degrees, that frog will eventually allow itself to be boiled to death.

At that Labor Day party, I definitely felt like that frog. The progression of circumstances slowly increased heat in my metaphoric pot. By the time I realized the degree to which my comfortably defined boundaries had been crossed, it was too late. I felt physically unable to act in a controlled and considerate way; I was at the boiling point.

Now, I know the frog story is a big myth. If an actual frog were tossed into boiling water, it would be so immediately scalded it wouldn't survive. And if allowed to hang out in tepid water, most frogs would no doubt hop out when the water became uncomfortably warm.

However, I still think it's a great allegory for how we make decisions. In my case, by neglecting to reinforce my boundaries at the beginning of the day, I had sealed my fate in the proverbial boiling pot.

If, on the other hand, I'd taken stock of the growing temperature of the water, I could have assessed the circumstances and determined the best course of action. Even when circumstances became intolerable, I still had the opportunity to act compassionately and in my best interest.

The more I've practiced mindfulness, the more I've also become aware of the fact that it's not enough to simply set or even articulate a boundary; we must also consistently enforce them. That requires a commitment to continually communicating boundaries. As a business owner, instead of blowing my lid, I have learned to say things like, "This isn't acceptable behavior," "I'm not satisfied with this work," or "I want you to shorten the delivery deadline on this project."

I have practiced the words I use to define my boundaries and reinforced my commitment by enforcing them. That's important. Every time we fail to enforce a boundary, we're telling the other person it's okay to ignore our boundaries. We're creating an invisible contract that says it's acceptable to disregard those boundaries. It allows the other person to believe we aren't serious about the boundaries we've set.

Conversely, by consistently and compassionately enforcing set boundaries, we're demonstrating we really mean it—and we're helping others build the habit of respecting articulated boundaries along the way.

Too often, I see individuals in supervisory roles establish but fail to enforce boundaries. If leaders expect a certain quality of work, punctuality, or a particular code of conduct, it's their responsibility to make that known to the employees and to address breaches of those expectations.

It's not enough to have it written in the handbook; it must become a part of the company culture. This goes for the ways in which the company operates, as well as defining the benchmarks for how the company hires, promotes, and fires employees.

For instance, let's say you own a bakery which opens at 6:00 a.m. A certain employee tends to wander into the shop around 6:15 a.m. You don't say anything at first and, instead, stew in your indignation while dealing with the line of customers awaiting their bagels and donuts.

Finally, on a particularly busy day, you reach the end of your rope and fire this habitually tardy employee. That's not

fair to the employee because up until that day, your unwillingness to reinforce the rules has indicated it's okay to come to
work fifteen or twenty minutes late.

Failing to enforce boundaries can also create apathy
amongst your other employees or team members. If several of
your employees always make it a point to arrive by 5:55 a.m.
but see there are no consequences for their tardy coworker,
they may well decide it's not worth making the extra effort
to get up early and get to work on time. They may also come
to resent the person who arrives late, or they may resent you
for allowing other workers to show up whenever they want.

An even more pervasive and destructive result could
be that your employees begin to fear they're breaching
other unstated boundaries and that, the next time you are
over-stressed and upset, they may be fired as well.

The same is true, of course, for family members as well.
Allowing a loved one to yell or speak in a passive-aggressive
way signals to them that you're okay with that continued
treatment. By drawing a clear line and articulating that line
in a firm but loving way, you are ultimately helping your loved
one treat you with greater respect and dignity.

By consistently enforcing boundaries and having clear
consequences for violations, we are reinforcing our values and
creating clear and consistent guidelines for behavior. In doing
so, we allow others to choose how they will act within the system we've outlined. They can choose to comply (or say "yes"),
rebel (or say "no"), or ask to compromise.

Always enforcing boundary breaches using the same words,
phrases, and methods of discipline creates an environment of
understanding, equality, and compassion. Repeatedly articulating and enforcing boundaries is also a form of self-care.

Of course, these days, the notion of "self-care" has become
overused and the subject of more than just a few unhelpful

memes on social media. Along the way, its true definition has been at least partially lost. It's time to take back that definition.

True self-care isn't indulging in a glass of chardonnay or a new face cream; it's asking for what you want and need. It's knowing what will make you feel safe and making the choices that support that state. It's respecting yourself enough that others around you show respect.

On the self-care pyramid, the base or foundation is setting and maintaining boundaries. As I have been known to tell my clients and friends, "'No' is a complete sentence." It's okay to allow a solid "no" response to be your final word on the subject.

Living your values and establishing good boundaries allows you to live a more authentic life. It can also mean stepping out of certain cultural expectations. You're not going to make everybody happy all of the time. This can be uncomfortable, particularly if it involves family members. Many of us were raised to believe family always comes first, or that we have certain family responsibilities.

When we find ourselves in a situation that compromises our values, one of the healthiest things we can do is step away long enough to reflect upon and become clear about the values we wish to maintain and those that will be compromised if we acquiesce to the expectations of others.

Cultural norms are powerful. As an individual, it's important to pause and choose what's best for you in the long run, particularly when it comes to personal health and well-being. Sometimes, that means making really hard decisions to forgo a commitment to family in order to prioritize a value like peace or psychological health.

Undoubtedly, those choices will occasionally be challenging. On the surface, they may appear to contradict beliefs held by our communities or the expectations placed on us by loved ones. Consequently, those decisions may also mean we feel compelled to modify or end relationships with friends and sometimes even family members.

One of the more unexpected and unpleasant side effects of a mindful life is it can, indeed, cause us to lose friends or family members along the way. I've heard multiple theories about why this may be. Personally, I think it's because we are growing as individuals and living more intentionally or consciously.

It may not be the case that those around us are on a similar path or trajectory. When, along with our growing self-knowledge, we begin to change our behaviors and our interactions with the people around us, we are breaking an implicit contract we have made with friends and family. We are changing the rules about the habits, beliefs, and behaviors that define our character to those around us.

Adopting a mindfulness practice is a little like forcing your family and friends to download an update for your operating system software. The program they clearly understood and could easily navigate has changed.

It will take loved ones time and practice to understand the new system. And it will be important for you to continue to enforce and embody your newly discovered values and boundaries so they have the opportunity to learn and accept this new system. Along the way, not everyone may agree to use this new operating system, which can create discord or distance. That can feel like a real loss.

However, it's also important to keep in mind that, sometimes, the best way to show compassion for someone is to let them go. There are all kinds of reasons not to engage with an individual, even if they are a close relative. Being able to recognize when relationships are causing us harm is another powerful tool we gain through a mindfulness practice. Letting go of that person is not an act of malice; it's an act of loving kindness—for both of you.

During the most heart-wrenching moments of loss, it can be helpful to remind ourselves that one of the best principles to live by is a commitment to making choices that promote positive mental health and a long, healthy life.

By prioritizing situations that reduce stress and increase satisfaction, we are ultimately investing in a high-value insurance policy, even if it means reassessing a few relationships along the way. This strategy minimizes some of the harmful effects of stress on the body and offers a huge payout in terms of joy and quality of life.

Staying In Our Own Lanes

In the days leading up to my marriage, my future father-in-law took me aside.

"Annamarie," he said. "Don't do anything now that you don't want to do for the rest of your life."

If you were to ask him today, my father-in-law would tell you he has no recollection of saying that. Nevertheless, that advice remains some of the best I've ever received. What I believe my father-in-law meant was any pattern I set early in my relationship with my husband would be very hard to break later on.

If I went into my new marriage picking up my husband's dirty socks, he'd come to expect that picking up his socks is on my job description as a wife. The same, of course, was true for me: a few complimentary oil changes from my new spouse, and I'd quickly assume I no longer had to worry about car maintenance.

We all make assumptions about our relationships on a daily basis. Each time we behave a certain way, we are ultimately making and reinforcing another contract with that person. As time goes on, these contracts can begin to feel ironclad.

One of the benefits of my mindfulness practice is I have become aware of these unspoken contracts and my participation in them. This new awareness has come with unexpected and powerful consequences in my life. It may for you, too. And that's okay.

A mindfulness practice can be a revolutionary experience. We practice mindfulness to learn and strengthen our values and to become the living embodiment of those values and our best selves. Once you identify the many minor ways you have been compromising your values, you will undoubtedly find you also begin to change your behaviors.

It's typical for those changes to be noticed by friends and family; it's also common for the people around you to react emotionally. Eventually, you may arrive at a place where you need to reassess these relationships. It's important to keep in mind that a mindfulness practice is really about self-discovery.

During this journey, we inevitably discover more about the people around us and how we interact. Early in a mindfulness journey, that can mean being curious about the choices we make and how people around us respond to those choices.

As our path continues, we often find ourselves changing and revising the rules we use to govern our relationships. Sometimes, this can really deepen and improve a relationship. Other times, it can compromise that relationship or even terminate it. And sometimes, that termination may be the very best thing—for everyone involved.

It takes real courage and conviction to put a stop to another person's destructive behavior. Happily, mindfulness can help on that front as well. For instance, just after I graduated from college, I worked as the manager of a retail store while I got my footing in the world of interior design.

It was the holiday season (a notoriously busy time for stores—especially those in a mall), and we were all feeling stressed by the Christmas shopping rush. One day, my supervisor called me into the back office and began berating me for a burnt-out lightbulb. I'd already given notice that I planned to leave my position and work full-time in design, but his behavior crossed a line I couldn't accept.

"No one has ever spoken to me like that," I told him. "And you will not be the first." With that, I walked out and never looked back.

That decision allowed me to live my values. I established a boundary, and I upheld it, even though doing so cost me one last paycheck, along with a positive reference from my boss. I was okay sacrificing both.

The fact is, not everyone is willing to honor our values or boundaries. But that doesn't mean we have to accept their unwillingness. Nor do we need to intercede on someone else's behalf. Far too often, I see people entering into negative, destructive contracts with their loved ones, their supervisors, or their coworkers. When I see that happening, I know not to get involved.

The best way I can demonstrate compassion is to know these two have established a contract. That contract, written with each tolerated destructive action, says the two individuals have at least tacitly agreed that their interaction is acceptable.

While I could wish they would see the situation differently, it's not my place to get involved. Nor is it okay for me to thrust my expectations for loving communication or a healthy relationship onto others. Not only might I make the situation worse, but I may also only bring further guilt and shame to the other people by addressing the situation.

Sitting on our hands and saying nothing can be a very difficult stance for some people to accept. Take a dear friend of mine, whom I'll call Denise. She's the kind of person who is always getting involved with other people's business because she believes it's the best way to show she cares.

I've tried to counsel Denise that her meddling actually comes across as disapproval, but she sees it otherwise. We've come to loggerheads over this in the past because she believes my lack of action means I don't care.

"But they're adults," I'll argue. "They can make their own choices. They know I'm here for them, and they'll ask for help if they need it."

I know from experience that inserting myself into a situation where a friend hasn't asked for help can go sideways in all kinds of ways. It usually leaves me feeling yucky and my friend feeling like I've overstepped or second-guessed them. It's hard not to get involved, and sometimes, I have to use significant willpower to refrain from offering unsolicited advice.

But I've learned to check those impulses and replace them with a simple and genuine offer: *If you ever want to talk, I'm here for you.* Even if the person never takes me up on that offer, I can content myself in knowing they received it. That is true compassion. It allows the recipient to take responsibility for what they need and reassures them they are not alone.

Of course, it's also true that many of us are challenged by the prospect of taking people up on their offer of help or support. We were taught to be self-reliant, to avoid being needy, to feel rejected if the other individual can't help. The reality, of course, is usually very different. Feeling empowered to ask for help is one of life's most important skills.

Chapter 6 Takeaways

- Our minds can become addicted to emotions, just like they can become reliant upon habits. These emotional addictions can even include unpleasant emotions, such as anger or sadness.

- One reason why these emotional addictions are so powerful is because of the chemical processes in our brain. Each time we experience a rush of adrenaline or dopamine (the so-called "feel good" hormone), our cells become accustomed to its effects. Eventually, they begin to crave that hormone, much like they might an addictive substance, such as alcohol or caffeine.

- The word "value" has several meanings. For the sake of our work here, I am defining it as "those individually held beliefs and principles that dictate our behavior." This is distinct from the idea of ethical or moral values, which often refer to a code of conduct established by a social group.

- To identify your own values, consider questions such as:

  - What are some of the attitudes or states that are most important to me?

  - When do I feel like my most authentic self?

  - What behaviors in others do I most admire? Conversely, what behaviors spark significant negative reactions in me?

- Oftentimes, we can tell when we aren't being true to our values because of the physical sensations in our body. If certain behaviors, such as gossiping or lying, create stress responses such as an elevated heart rate, feelings of anxiety, tightness in your chest, or nervousness, that's a good indication you're behaving contrary to one of your values. Similarly, when we experience joy or peace, that's a good indication we are behaving in a way aligned with our values.

- Embodying our values often requires us to establish boundaries with others. Doing so can be facilitated by practicing the three C's: *clarify, communicate,* and *commit.*

- In addition to setting boundaries, we must also be prepared to maintain them. This can often be at least—if not more—challenging than establishing the boundaries. However, every time we fail to enforce a boundary, we are signaling to others that it is okay to disregard or cross that boundary.

- Sometimes, part of the process of identifying our values and boundaries means we find ourselves in conflict with friends and loved ones. In some cases, this may mean the safest and healthiest choice is to limit or terminate contact with them.

Chapter 6 Exercises

Formal Mindfulness Practice

A Moment of Self Love

With this exercise, I offer you a moment in which to focus on self-care, self-compassion, self-discovery, and personal healing.

So, let's begin. As you read through these cues, let your focus soften, retaining a sense of the space around you. Move your attention inward and allow your awareness to include your interior world: your thoughts, physical sensations, emotions, and intuitions, as well as the sights, sounds, tastes, smells, and textures around you.

Your eyes can be open or closed—whatever feels right to you in the moment.

Whenever you're ready, straighten your spine and gently lift your head up, through the crown of your head, toward the sky.

Pause, take a deep breath in, then let it out. Notice where you might be tense, and gently caress those areas of tension with your breath.

Now, balance your feet on the floor or your sitting bones on the seat. Pause to notice if there is anything in your body and mind that wants to be noticed in this space

Take a deep breath in, and then let it out. Take another breath in, then out. Pause for a moment after the exhale: what do you notice?

Take another breath in and out, then pause again. Listen for the moment when your breath is momentarily suspended, and observe the sensations there.

Take a deep breath in and out, and pause again, repeating the process.

When you're ready, take another breath in and out. Wiggle your fingers and your toes, and open your eyes if they are closed.

Take a moment to send gratitude to yourself and all the things that align in order for you to be present in this moment and remember you can take this practice with you wherever you go.

Informal Mindfulness Practice

Press Pause

This is an exercise that encourages a moment of deep awareness. It's a super powerful practice to engage when you notice you've been triggered or feel your emotions rising. It can be done at any time and in any situation throughout the day. You can be standing, seated, or lying down.

To begin, set the intention to move into your mindfulness practice. This is as simple as making a choice in the moment to switch to noticing yourself and the world around you in a deeper, richer way.

Take a conscious breath in. Inhale with the intention to feel your breath as it moves through and with your body.

Release your breath. Relax the parts of your body that want to relax.

When you're ready, focus your eyes. Look around you, like a photographer looking for the perfect photograph: notice the light as it stands, reflects, and glides through the room, along with colors, contrasts, textures, and movement. Move your attention to the people: see their faces, hands, body position, and possibly the movement of their mouths as they form words. Simply spend a few moments seeing the space and the people around you.

Now, tune into your ears, focusing your attention on everything you hear happening around you. You may hear the hum of a refrigerator or the sound of someone's voice. Resist the temptation to judge, assess, change, or fix; simply acknowledge that everything you notice is occurring here and now, and whatever you notice is a part of your experience in this moment. Focus your attention on the vibration, texture, and the felt sensations of what you hear.

When you're ready, move your attention to the conversation in your head. Hear your thoughts as if you are listening to a podcast, with a degree of separation between you and your reasonings. Simply listen as you would to the musings of a best friend.

Now, when you're ready, notice the sensations and emotions in your body. You may see them as a color, hear them as a hum, or feel them as a flutter or a vibration.. Whatever you notice is valid, and if you notice nothing, that is also fine.

Finally, take a conscious breath in and out.

Repeat this mantra:

Breathing in, I calm my body and mind.
Breathing out, I smile.

··· 7 ···

Living the Mindful Life

GROWING UP, I was educated in parochial schools, where we were taught human behavior could be divided into two buckets: good actions and bad actions.

As far as the priests and nuns were concerned, we students were either going to become good girls or bad girls, destined for heaven or hell, depending upon the decisions we made and our ability (or willingness) to follow their moral code. I deeply internalized these lessons at an early age, along with a view of life that distilled everything into black and white.

It wasn't until I enrolled in a theology class at my small Catholic college that this worldview began to change. I didn't sign up for that course with any vested interest in theology but rather because the nun who taught the course was one of the most fascinating humans I've ever met.

She structured the class as an introduction to world religions and explicitly stressed the commonalities between them. It was my first exposure to comparative mythology, and I was blown away not only by the range of beliefs but also by how many different cultures shared important underlying ideology.

The other thing that really struck me about the class was the range of students taking it. Having grown up in parochial schools, I had completed all twelve years of my primary education with essentially the same 73 students. They, in turn, all came from backgrounds remarkably similar to my own. College was a different ecosystem entirely. Suddenly, I was surrounded by people who looked and behaved very differently than I did. I loved that, too.

One of the students who really stood out in my theology course was an eccentric young woman who always seemed larger than life and who asked the most intense, intellectual questions of our professor. Growing up, I'd always been the kind of student who was curious but too timid to ask questions. This girl, on the other hand, clearly wasn't afraid to ask *anything*. And no matter what line her inquiry took, the instructor always answered each and every question with enthusiasm and patience.

Watching the two of them interact taught me a lot about the value of curiosity and participation. I had always thought questioning a teacher would either reveal my ignorance or make it seem as if I were questioning the instructor's authority.

This vivacious classmate of mine showed me the very real ways that engagement can demonstrate not only a commitment to learning but also an open mind ready to consider whatever is offered. That realization was revolutionary for me. And in some very real ways, it laid the foundation for a lifetime of mindfulness work, particularly with regards to mindfulness's emphasis on cultivating curiosity and an openness to exploring ourselves and our environment.

I wish I could say the story ends there. Unfortunately, my classmate had harder lessons to teach as well. Midway through that school year, I learned she had committed suicide. The news shook me to the core. Although we hadn't really known each other, I'd come to see my classmate as having a superpower: the ability to explore any subject in order to discover a deeper truth.

She never gave any indication she was depressed or experiencing a mental health crisis (at least none I detected). The idea that this young woman whom I'd grown to admire would take her own life sent me into my own kind of depression.

Here was this person who seemed to embody the ability not only to be curious but also to be open to the whole wide world. She didn't appear to suffer from the same limitations I'd internalized throughout my upbringing, and she seemed prepared to embrace whatever came her way. I couldn't fathom how anyone so bold and brave could succumb to the kind of despair that would lead to suicide.

Since then, I've learned a lot more about mental health. However, all these years later, I still get choked up thinking about her life and the loss of her presence in the world. I wish I could thank that classmate for the awakening she brought to me.

After I emerged from my initial sadness about her suicide, I found myself looking for ways to embody my classmate's openness and curiosity. Along the way, I found I also had an unquenchable desire to learn more about the human condition.

That prompted me to begin examining my own habits and beliefs: *What were the real reasons I was afraid to ask questions? Why was I not able to express myself outwardly? What happens when we try to hide or mask our feelings rather than invite them in?*

I couldn't know it at the time, but in that quest for understanding, I had taken my first real step toward living a mindful life.

Cultivating Awareness and Acceptance

Mindfulness in practice is really all about setting an intention to be curious, to be aware, and to accept. If you can make good on that intention, you've succeeded at establishing your own successful mindfulness practice.

It really is that simple. Of course, getting to a place where we remember and engage that intention, rather than slipping back into old judgments, can feel easier said than done. But, like so many other things, it really does get easier with practice and time.

Mindfulness begins with a willingness to be open, even to ourselves and the thoughts and feelings we experience. Mary Oliver, one of my very favorite poets, illustrates this concept beautifully in "Wild Geese." That poem opens with the line, "You do not have to be good." As she explains a few lines later, "You only have to let the soft animal of your body / love what it loves."

I just adore that image. A brilliant mindfulness practitioner herself, Oliver understood we aren't merely our thoughts and feelings, and we can let our monkey brains do all their monkey things without *becoming* those thoughts and ideas.

As someone raised in a religion that insisted on the idea of *good*, having someone as thoughtful and wise as Mary Oliver tell me I can surrender that concept in favor of what is *real* was intensely liberating. So much so, in fact, that I still have a strong emotional response every time I read that poem.

I think that's in large part because I feel like Mary Oliver is walking next to me and reminding me it's okay. As someone who is personally challenged by ideas of acceptance, that reminder goes a long way toward helping in my own mindfulness journey.

This concept of acceptance is a very important one for any mindfulness practice. Especially initially, a mindfulness practice is bound to make us aware not only of our best selves, but also the selves we're not so proud of. The more conscious you become of your thoughts and feelings, the more you'll begin to notice the times you feel resentful, jealous, aggravated, or impatient.

It's important to keep in mind that that doesn't necessarily (or even probably) mean you're experiencing more of those emotions. Instead, they're just migrating into your awareness. Go ahead and let them; like all other thoughts, they will pass like clouds. By simply becoming aware of these thoughts (and the degree to which they do not define you), you have already begun to liberate yourself from any hold they may exert.

Building our capacity to pay attention in this way can feel like a daunting task. From a young age, we're told to sit still and pay attention, first by our parents and elders and then by our teachers. However, few (if any) of these adults ever actually taught us *how* to sit still and pay attention.

Most of us were never offered exercises or tools to help us focus our minds and quiet our bodies, which made it all the more challenging to do either. Life in the digital age has only made this more difficult.

A recent study found that average Americans check their smartphones about 144 times a day. Nearly 90 percent of those surveyed say they do so within the first ten minutes of waking up, and three-quarters said they also do so while using the toilet. The same number said they rarely, if ever, wait more than five minutes before picking up their phones after receiving a notification.[1] No wonder many of us feel like we have a real attention deficit!

Mindfulness teaches us how to build attention and focus. One particularly effective way to do so is through meditation. As I explained in Chapter 1, meditation is not about transcending our thoughts, nor is it about the ability to focus singularly on a mantra or the great oneness of the university.

Meditation is really about cultivating our awareness in the present moment. As Jon Kabat Zinn puts it, "Meditation is an invitation to just drop in and experience the actuality of our experience." One easy way we can do so is choosing an anchor, such as the conscious awareness of our breath. Some people like to choose an easy mantra they can quietly recite, such as "I am in the present," or even just a single word like "here" or "now."

No matter how well you manage to focus on that breath or mantra, it's inevitable that other thoughts and observations are going to creep in. You might hear the sound of a car driving by or your dogs barking at a delivery person. Perhaps you begin to think about all the tasks standing between you and the end of the day, or you begin to worry about how your kids are doing or whether that new bump on your arm might be cancerous.

That's okay.

Simply acknowledge that thought and then return to your breathing. And remember: it's important not to judge yourself (or your brain) for this wandering. Just remind yourself that's what brains like to do, and then return to the breath.

Sometimes, I like to do this by gently teasing my brain: *Silly mind,* I might say, *there you go again, making grocery lists and multi-tasking.* An observation like that reminds me to respond to my monkey brain with loving kindness rather than judgment or criticism.

And remember: the repetition of shifting our focus from thinking to an anchor (the anchor can be the breath, felt sensations in the body, a mantra, etc.) is all it takes to build new neural pathways in the form of beneficial habits and beliefs we can use as we navigate our day. Just as importantly, keep in mind that a month, a year, or even a decade of meditation is not going to turn you into a saint any more than it's going to make you an expert yogi.

I learned this the hard way. Not long after I began teaching meditation, I committed to a silent retreat. By then, I was a certified yoga instructor who had also become self-taught in the practice of meditation, so I figured the four-day retreat would be a breeze. I arrived with a suitcase overflowing with ego and was certain I was as good a meditator as any instructor at the retreat. Holy cow, did I have a lot to learn!

The minute I walked into the door of the retreat center, I immediately felt like a fish out of water. Most of the participants were there to complete their advanced yoga teacher training, and they looked the part. They were young, beautiful, and super-fit Instagram influencers.

To make matters worse, I didn't know a soul there, so I instantly felt like an awkward new kid on the first day of third grade. Those feelings, in turn, brought up a lot of fear in me, and I soon found myself back in so many of the mental patterns I'd developed while at parochial school—all that self-talk about *good* or *bad* and *right* or *wrong*.

To make matters worse, I soon learned an essential truth about mindfulness meditation: because it requires us to really pay attention to our thoughts and feelings, it can bring all of our fears and insecurities to the surface, especially when we can't distract ourselves with the usual crutches like binge-watching movies or digging into a wheel of Guggisberg cheese. In other words, there was nothing I could do to escape the stories my mind was telling me.

The particular meditation retreat I'd signed up for was also a *silent* retreat, and, in addition to not speaking, we weren't supposed to interact with each other using body language. As a result, the other participants and I mostly moved from sessions to meals with our gazes down, often not even making eye contact.

As the "winner of the kindest senior award" who has learned to use a friendly smile as a way to mask my discomfort, I'd lost yet another coping mechanism I'd developed over the years. This lack of communication also meant I had even more time and space to wallow in the insecurities that had arisen the minute I arrived at the center. Without any of my traditional modes of creating self-comfort, I was left to the stark realities of my thoughts and feelings.

Over the next few days, I had plenty of opportunities to notice my insecurities and how they were affecting my experience in different situations. One of the ways I've always compensated for feeling insecure is by taking a leadership role.

At school, I'd take charge during small group work or be the friend who was always hosting the party or planning the weekend adventure. As a business owner, I've derived a lot of self-worth from being the person making the big decisions. During that four-day retreat, I found myself struggling to play the role of the recipient student when I'd become so accustomed to serving as a teacher.

Without realizing it, I began looking for ways I could take charge.

I was sure I'd finally found that opportunity during a communal meal. At this particular retreat, our lunches and dinners were served buffet-style, and one afternoon, my side of the buffet line ran out of plates before we'd all gotten our lunch. There it was: the leadership moment I'd been waiting for. I approached a member of the kitchen staff.

"I'm sorry," I said in my best kind-CEO voice. "There are no plates on the far side. Will you please restock the buffet line?"

That guy looked at me like I was totally out to lunch. And as I gazed around the room, I could see my fellow participants were totally bewildered as well. This was a silent retreat. There was no immediate emergency because on the other side of the table was a stack of plates easily within reach. So why was this woman squawking about plates? I began to ask myself the same question. And just as I did, any sense of accomplishment I had was soon replaced with total, mortal embarrassment. *Oh my god*, I thought to myself. *I am a total doofus!*

Luckily, I still had plenty of time at the retreat to reflect upon my decision to speak up (and the subsequent feelings of shame). Once I got past all of the self-recrimination, I began to consider the real ways I'd become stifled by my habits and beliefs. Instead of acknowledging my insecurities, I'd used initiative and a need to control to hide those unpleasant emotions.

By insisting upon a leadership role (whether or not one was required), I'd also built a set of armor for myself that made real intimacy difficult, especially since I used that armor to avoid my own vulnerability.

These were hard lessons to learn, but thank goodness I did. That awareness led me to a place of acceptance and a desire for a new, better path.

I began to understand the true cost of my impulse to control everything or make it perfect. I noticed when I was triggered and was relying upon habituated responses rather than choosing intentionality. As hard as that retreat felt at times, it revealed some important truths about myself that I needed to confront if I wanted to form better relationships, both with the people I love and with myself.

Recognizing those truths can be a painful process. And it can be tempting to avoid the discomfort that comes with self-exploration. As scary and potentially unpleasant as that experience might seem, I encourage you to embrace it. We may not always like what we see in the mirror, but being willing to look is the first step toward acknowledging our past thoughts and experiences as well as the person we are becoming.

That retreat also taught me about the value of undertaking a mindfulness journey in community. Had I not attended that workshop, had I not been willing to take on the role of student, I would not have had the opportunity for the incredible growth and awareness I gained over those four days.

Attending mindfulness workshops, working with qualified teachers, and joining a community of other mindfulness practitioners are all opportunities for deep, lasting work, and they set up an accountability framework that makes it easier to uphold our commitments to practice.

As you begin your own mindfulness journey, consider ways in which you can undertake it with others. Whether it's committing to a weekly yoga class, attending a Quaker meeting, or participating in a local mindfulness meditation group, being with others can go a long way toward helping you establish a practice that works.

Make a Training Plan (And Stick to It!)

Earlier in the book, I described my decision to complete a triathlon and the surprising emotions evoked in my cycling class. That race had other important lessons to teach me as well. My decision to compete in the triathlon was born largely out of a desire to get out of a funk and make important decisions about the next chapter in my life. I knew I needed focus to do both, and I thought the training required to complete the race would help me develop that attribute.

Up until my decision to register for this race, I'd led a fairly sedentary life. Consequently, I had no idea how to prepare for an event that would require me to swim, bike, and run. After a little time on the Internet, I bought a copy of *Triathlon Revolution: Training, Technique, and Inspiration* by Terri Schneider and committed to the step-by-step training it prescribed.

For me, the most valuable part of the book was a four-week schedule that dictated each day's workout. Day One of the first week was "Stretch: 15 minutes." I thought, "I can do that!" Subsequent days might include a thirty-minute run or a forty-five-minute bike ride. And even as the workouts became longer, each week also included one day where all that was required was a fifteen-minute stretch.

That plan seemed super doable—or at least it did until I began to contemplate the reality of the swim workouts. I've always loved being in water, but my version of swimming is usually a very loose interpretation of the breaststroke that leaves my hair dry and doesn't require me to keep my face in the water. Committing to the pool workouts proved difficult.

I'd always known I prefer sitting around and having intellectual conversations over taking a fitness class, and one of my explanations has always been that I lack willpower, especially where athletic pursuits are concerned. I'd just always believed that willpower was an innate attribute—we're either born with it, or we're not.

I felt certain I'd just missed out on the willpower gene, which is why I'd never managed to maintain a strict diet or regular trips to the gym. After I committed to the triathlon, I knew that belief wasn't going to work anymore.

So I bought yet another book: Kelly McGonigal's wonderful *The Willpower Instinct: How Self-Control Works, Why it Matters, and What You Can Do To Get More of It.* A health psychologist and lecturer at Stanford University, McGonigal explains the very real ways we can build a greater capacity for willpower in our daily lives through mindfulness, self-awareness, and self-care.

For a long time, I believed that willpower was genetic— something we either got or didn't get at birth, like the ability to whistle or the tendency to freckle after a day in the sun. It wasn't until I began studying mindfulness that I realized willpower is really more like a great cup of coffee. We all have the same-sized mug (one of those super-sized soup bowls the French use for *cafe au lait*), and it's up to us how much we pour into it.

A consistent mindfulness meditation practice helps you increase the levels in your cup and the volume of willpower in your life. Mindfulness practices, such as identifying and naming emotions, body scans, and circle breathing, strengthen your resilience and ability to activate patience. It also builds your emotional intelligence library, creating a bottomless cup of willpower you can use even in times of stress.

This analogy of the coffee mug has been revolutionary for me, particularly when it comes to understanding habits like my fondness for aggressive driving. As soon as I understood that determining the volume in my cup was ultimately up to me, I also realized I was in control.

Meditation and mindfulness help us practice willpower by consistently moving our focus from our thinking thoughts and back to our anchor (like our breath, a mantra, or the felt sensations in our body). These practices also make it easier to increase the volumes in our metaphoric coffee cups by strengthening the muscles we use to pause for a moment and be reflective rather than immediately acting whenever we're triggered.

Every time we practice mindfulness, we strengthen our willpower. That, in turn, makes it easier for us to exert the physical energy needed to shift from reacting out of habit to consciously choosing an action or response that is in keeping with our values.

Strengthening our ability to draw on willpower allows us to show greater compassion for ourselves in those moments. Knowing when we might need compassion is also an important skill.

For instance, I know I'm a person who tends to totally overschedule myself. Left to my own devices, I'll plan one meeting for 9 a.m. and another for 10 a.m. without acknowledging that the two are a twenty-minute drive from one another. That kind of poor planning sets me up to fail—I'll wake up in the morning already feeling stressed about my day, knowing I'll spend chunks of time racing around in a heightened state of agitation.

When it comes to willpower, that kind of overscheduling makes it more difficult to be present and mindful. To counteract that impulse, I now know to schedule appointments for fifty minutes rather than an hour, so I'll at least have ten minutes to reset.

Sleep is another trigger for me, as are diet, exercise, and meditation. When I'm invested in those practices, I know I'll have an easier time regulating my levels of stress and won't need to draw upon my willpower as much as I would if I were agitated. That's because these practices tap into the powers of the parasympathetic nervous system.

Most of us are born with innately effective parasympathetic nervous systems well suited for countering the stress mechanisms associated with the sympathetic nervous system. The challenges arise when we allow our habits and beliefs (including thoughts, judgments, worries, insecurities, expectations, and assumptions) to interfere with the parasympathetic nervous system's functioning.

When that happens, it becomes more difficult to be mindful and fully present to what's happening, both inside us and in our worlds. Simply understanding the power of these habits and beliefs is like drinking your amazing cup of hot coffee and having the level never decrease. And when we recognize we are being controlled and cramped by habits and beliefs, it's like being gifted a bottomless willpower mug.

It's glorious.

Meditation and mindfulness help us practice willpower and keep our mug filled to the brim. It gives us the power to pause and make a deliberate choice. It also fosters greater self-compassion. In the moments where we still find ourselves being reactive, we can pause and reflect upon what is happening and why.

For me, that includes the ability to have inner dialogues of empathy and understanding—conversations like: *Well, Annamarie, you've had a hectic travel schedule. You haven't been sleeping well, you've been eating out a lot, and you haven't found time to exercise. Of course, you're more easily triggered. How can you prepare differently so you may do better next time?*

That kind of internal pep talk goes a long way toward curtailing my critical thoughts and, instead, allows me to be compassionate about my own experience. The key is I talk to myself as I would to someone I love and care about, someone I wish to see thrive. I treat myself as I would my best friend.

That includes making choices that feed my mindfulness practice.

On a day when I've gotten enough sleep, had my oatmeal for breakfast, and left for work with plenty of time to get there, I have the capacity to be mindful of growing tension or stress before it begins to consume me. When I feel angry, for instance, there's a tingling in my scalp, almost like it's electrified. I can also feel a tightness in my ribcage, back, and shoulders that seems to pitch my whole body forward.

If I'm able to recognize those signals early, I can acknowledge them and be curious about their root cause rather than allowing them to control me. But that takes real effort, so I try to set myself up for success by going to bed early, eating healthful food, and making time for exercise and meditation.

I encourage you to do the same. If you haven't gotten enough sleep, if you haven't exercised or eaten well, if you haven't been moderate in your consumption of alcohol or caffeine or even sugar, practicing mindfulness can feel next to impossible.

For that reason alone, it's important to commit to self-care as part of your mindfulness journey. If you've ever flown commercially, you've undoubtedly heard a flight attendant's safety briefing, which includes the instructions to always fix your own oxygen mask before helping others around you. That's a good metaphor to remember, not just for a new mindfulness practice but for life in general.

In the case of my triathlon, I knew the best way I could serve myself was by committing to following the training schedule in my book. I worked with a swim coach, increased my distance until I could swim the breaststroke for a mile in the pool, and was overjoyed when I completed the race.

Since then, I've gone on to finish multiple triathlons, and I'm very proud to say I've always finished in the middle of the pack (my very favorite place to be). Most importantly, I have gained a tremendous sense of accomplishment knowing I could overcome perceived limitations by challenging gently used muscles and cultivating skills I already had deep inside.

Committing to a mindfulness practice is just like triathlon training. We all have the capacity to become more open, more curious, and more aware. Most of us just need commitment, tools, and an accountability structure to do so.

In my own life, I find it very supportive to plan for both *formal* and *informal* mindfulness practice. As you've seen in the exercises offered in previous chapters, formal mindfulness practice is like the gym workouts prescribed by my triathlon training book: it's setting a timer and sitting on your meditation cushion for twenty minutes each day, participating in a weekly mindfulness group, or attending a regular yoga class.

In that regard, formal mindfulness usually has a set beginning and end. Knowing you're in a safe place for a specific amount of time can really help develop your mindfulness muscles. Formal mindfulness practice also requires a commitment and intention to practice. You have to decide to participate, put it on your calendar, and get to your appointment on time. Doing so has the added benefit of building a habit that, in turn, requires less energy and draws less on your cup of willpower: the willpower you'll need to practice mindfulness throughout your day.

Informal mindfulness is equally important. It's the "throughout-your-day mindfulness," those little moments that pop up, sometimes unexpectedly and invite us to be present. Informal mindfulness requires pausing when you're triggered to move into a state of presence and awareness. It's also intentionally moving your attention to your five senses and discovering everything that's happening in the world around you.

Several years ago, I was fortunate enough to attend a yoga class taught by an instructor who really understood the power of informal mindfulness. At the start of each class, she'd remind us to put our cell phones on airplane mode. Invariably, someone in the class would forget, and just as we were settling into a pose, someone's phone would go off, often blaring a campy song or ringtone. My impulse in such moments would be to feel deeply annoyed that someone had forgotten to heed our teacher's instructions. But she had a different take on the situation.

"Every time a phone rings, it's an opportunity to practice," she'd tell us. "The next time you hear someone else's phone, use it as an invitation to pause for thirty seconds."

Those simple instructions turned a perennial frustration of mine into a welcome relief. Now, whenever I hear a canned guitar riff or electronic chirp of crickets on someone's phone, I use it as an opportunity to be fully present.

I take a few moments to observe my thoughts and the sensations in my body: *What do I see and feel? What emotions am I experiencing? What does it feel like to be supported by the earth (or a boardroom chair or park bench)? What is going on around me at this moment?*

Asking and answering questions such as these allows us to drop into a deep state of awareness and to become fully present. You can also create opportunities for this kind of informal practice by leaving Post-it Notes around your house, identifying certain sounds like a microwave chirp as an invitation to breathe, or even by inviting friends to text you with a reminder.

Personally, I like to use red traffic lights while I'm driving, along with lines at the grocery store, for this kind of informal practice as well.

When it comes down to it, pretty much everything in our daily lives can become an opportunity to practice mindfulness, so long as we are willing to make the commitment. Once we have made that promise to ourselves, the effects can feel remarkable—and sometimes even comical.

To this day, I have a Pavlovian response to other people's phones. I can be mid-sentence and deep in conversation when the sound of a ringtone will compel me to stop and take a couple of cleansing breaths. It may confuse the person who's waiting for me to finish my thought, but even just that one intentional moment is a powerful opportunity to drop into a state of deep awareness.

Just remember that awareness also takes practice and willpower.

I also find visualization techniques helpful. When I'm about to project negative energy in the form of hurtful language, pointed gazes, or eye rolls, I take a few conscious breaths and imagine myself retracting that negative energy and allowing it to dissipate with each exhale. Some days, that's easier than others.

The fact is, we can never fully undo previously established pathways inside our brains. Ask any recovering drug or alcohol addict, and they will tell you the act of staying sober is a daily practice. Walking a new path becomes easier every day, and yet, the established habitual path always remains, which is why practicing mindfulness and continuing to develop your willpower is a lifelong exercise.

Albert Einstein once said that *we can't solve a problem by using the same thinking that created it* (I'm using italics here because that's actually a paraphrase of a much larger quote).

What I think he meant is we have to shift our perspectives and get away from our old beliefs and habits in order to find workable solutions.

Mindfulness allows us to do that more easily by giving us a practice that encourages us to examine those perspectives. Practicing to pause, to be curious, and to resist judging ourselves and others gives us the opportunity to surrender the beliefs and habits that no longer serve us and move, step by step, toward living our best self.

Chapter 7 Takeaways

- At its core, a mindfulness practice is about being curious, aware, and open to exploring both ourselves and our environment.

- Like all other worthwhile pursuits, mindfulness becomes easier with practice and repetition.

- Mindfulness also requires us to accept ourselves as we are, even when we aren't being our best selves. The key is to notice these moments and reflect upon them without slipping into judgment.

- An often unexpected side effect of mindfulness is we become more aware of unpleasant truths about our behaviors and beliefs. It's of the nature of the mind to pass judgment in such moments. Resist that urge. Instead, merely acknowledge these moments as part of the process of becoming your best self.

- Recognizing that the mind loves to think random thoughts, even when we're trying to meditate, is an important part of the acceptance process. Each time we find our mind straying or thinking unhelpful thoughts, all we need to do is to return to our anchor. This simple act of returning our attention is all it takes to build greater neuroplasticity and beneficial neurological connections.

- Willpower is like a coffee mug: we can learn to fill and refill it in time. Mindfulness helps us create a bigger mug and keep it brimming with a delicious latte or fragrant chai.

- One of the best ways to cultivate greater willpower is to begin with self-care. Making sure you're filling your body with nutritious food, you're staying hydrated and getting enough rest, and you're making time to exercise and relax are all key contributors both to enhancing your willpower and developing your mindfulness practice.

- Another way to advance your mindfulness practice is to establish a regular schedule or training plan. This can include setting regular alerts on a smart device, committing to a regular yoga class or meditation program, or making time to meditate or practice breathing exercises at the beginning or end of each day.

Chapter 7 Exercises

Formal Mindfulness Practice

A Meditation on Unpleasant Emotions

This meditation is adopted from a series of meditations intended to promote positivity developed by Courtney Ackerman, an expert in mental health and positive psychology and the author of several books on the subject. It is intended to help dissipate negative emotions and to create the distance needed to observe these feelings without judgment. As with any of the exercises in this book, use this meditation only if you feel safe and supported. If you are someone who has experienced significant trauma and its effects, it may be best to consult or practice with a trained mental health provider.

1. Sit in a comfortable position. Take a moment to notice the feel of the floor or chair against your body and how your body feels in this posture.

2. Take several cleansing breaths, feeling the air as it enters and exits your lungs.

3. When you feel ready, think back to a recent moment when you felt an unpleasant emotion, such as anger, jealousy, or resentment. This exercise is most effective if you choose a relatively inconsequential moment (such as being cut off by another driver or being asked to stay and work overtime at your job rather than a major episode, such as a breakup or news of a betrayal by someone you love).

4. Replay this moment, focusing on how the emotion manifested in your body. Did you feel a tightness in your chest? Did you see red? Did you feel an urge to fight or flee? How did that urge present itself?

5. As you conduct this physical scan, pay attention to any thoughts or judgments that may appear. As they arise, simply notice them and allow them to pass. To help in this release, you might say something like, "I see you, shame," or you might simply thank your mind for trying to protect you. The important thing here is you observe the thoughts without accepting or becoming them.

6. Release the unpleasant emotion. You can do this in a variety of ways. One such example is a simple mantra: "Breathing in, I acknowledge this emotion. Breathing out, I let it go." You might also consider some gentle movement, such as pushing it out from your chest as if you were passing a basketball to a teammate.

7. As you feel the emotion dissipate, notice any physical changes in your body. Does your heart rate slow? Do you feel cooler or less tight? Take a moment to enjoy these changes and the clarity they bring.

Informal Mindfulness Practice

Fifty Things

This exercise is often employed by therapists and mediators as a way of de-escalating intense or triggering situations. The process is simple: when you feel yourself becoming anxious, frustrated, or otherwise reactive, take a moment to return to your physical surroundings.

Using your five senses, take an inventory of these surroundings, pointing out or naming fifty specific things (if you are in traffic, for instance, you might begin by noting a song on the radio, the reading of your odometer, a billboard next to you, etc.).

This exercise also works well during interpersonal conflict as well. If you and a loved one find yourself in an increasingly volatile or emotional exchange, pause to notice fifty (or twenty or ten) things.

Another exercise that can also build connection is to take turns noticing something specific in your surroundings, such as the ticking of the clock or the color of a pillow. After you name this thing, your loved one should then take the time to observe it and name it as well. Then, they can observe the next thing, and you can respond the same way.

••• 8 •••
Fostering Compassion and Gratitude

MANY YEARS AGO, I facilitated a women's group rooted in ideas of egalitarianism and open discourse. To help encourage free expression, I borrowed the practice of the talking circle, which first originated among Indigenous tribes in what is now the American Midwest. Simply put, the talking circle is based on the idea that everyone comes to the space with an equal voice and can only speak when they are holding the "talking piece" (traditionally, a symbolic object brought by the facilitator or circle keeper).

In our particular group, we used this tradition to foster an environment where the person holding the talking piece could speak their mind and say whatever they wanted to about what was happening in their world. There were no time limits; rather, the person could speak her truth until there was nothing left to say, then hand the talking piece to the woman sitting next to her.

I created other policies as well. Talking circles were not supposed to be dialogues, debates, or discussions. They were an opportunity for participants to express their thoughts fully and without interruption; listening quietly was a gift the rest of us could give to the speaker.

Everything said in this circle was confidential and couldn't be discussed later unless the speaker herself chose to bring it up. I insisted on a very strict adherence to this rule. Our job as circle participants was to listen, not to respond. We weren't there to come up with solutions or offer alternative perspectives; we weren't even there to provide comfort and solace.

That last rule *really* challenged a lot of the participants. Most of us had been raised to do nurturing things when someone was upset or hurt, whether it was offering a hug or a tissue, patting someone's shoulder, or making affirming comments.

At first, refraining from those sorts of comforting gestures was hard for many circle participants. But I stuck to my guns about the rule for several reasons. The real goal of the circle was to allow people's emotions to exist and be expressed however they needed to be. I wanted a place where those emotions could be real and immediate and raw, without anyone acting to smooth them over.

I've come to believe our culture is, as a whole, profoundly uneasy with other people's difficult emotions. Seeing someone in distress makes us uncomfortable. Oftentimes, our attempts to comfort someone are really about our own desire for relief from that distress. We want the difficult emotions to go away because sitting with them feels yucky and uncomfortable. We hand the person a tissue because we don't like being with someone who is crying.

I wanted our time together to serve as a corrective for those habituated responses. So, in our talking circle, tissues were always available, but it was up to the person speaking to decide if and when she needed one.

Sitting quietly with someone else's discomfort without moving to change it was a real stretch for many of the participants, including me. But we stuck with it, and as more people had the opportunity to share, I think everyone began to see the real power of being able to narrate their feelings and experiences.

We had succeeded in creating a space where our collective silence was the one and only place where someone could speak freely and feel truly heard. In that regard, the talking circle really was a very special gift we could give one another.

When I think about compassion, I think about that talking circle. Oftentimes, we tend to confuse compassion with concepts like sympathy or pity. I find the Latin root of the word a useful way of distinguishing this very important behavior. The word "compassion" literally translates as "suffering together."

And not just any kind of suffering but the suffering of Jesus Christ as he was crucified. Whether or not you subscribe to a Judeo-Christian faith, I think that image is a particularly powerful way to describe the act of being compassionate: it's the idea of bearing witness to profound suffering.

Developing a capacity for compassion is an integral part of the mindfulness journey. In order to practice, we must be able to sit with discomfort—both ours and that of those around us.

Mindfulness is about the willingness to hold our unpleasant feelings of grief or sadness, anger or betrayal, without looking away or acting in habitual ways to mask them with distractions. It's about breaking out of our habits of downplaying or avoiding our unpleasant feelings and, instead, allowing them to be exactly as they are.

May I Be Happy: Why Self-Compassion Matters (And How to Find It)

When I began my own mindfulness journey, I didn't even understand the concept of self-compassion, let alone know how to practice it. I was living squarely in the judgment zone—full of negative self-talk and constant internal criticism for what I felt certain were my many shortcomings.

It took time (and a lot of personal work) before I began to understand the value of living in a place of non-judgment. This acceptance of our present state is the first step toward developing self-compassion. Rather than assigning a value to our thoughts and feelings, we can simply acknowledge them as real without bestowing them with meaning.

For instance, if I have a series of uncharitable thoughts for the driver in front of me on a busy morning, the old Annamarie might have then begun to fall down a rabbit hole of self-criticism: *I'm a terrible person for getting impatient with an elderly driver. I should try to be more charitable. As a mindfulness teacher, I'm supposed to be better than this.*

However, if I'm acting from a place of self-compassion, my thinking might go more like, *There goes my brain again, getting all worked up by other people's driving.* And that's it. I acknowledge my frustration is real, but I don't judge myself for it.

One of the reasons I personally have a difficult time with self-compassion is because of the different beliefs I've accumulated over the years. Some were imposed upon me by my family and religion; others were encouraged by my alter ego, Little Miss Perfect. Together, they've conspired to make me believe I always need to be my best and to be particularly hard on myself when I fall short.

For me, an important part of mindfulness is recognizing when those beliefs are influencing my thoughts, ideas, and, ultimately, my behaviors. Mindfulness encourages us to be curious rather than critical when these thoughts appear.

As soon as I'm in a place dictated by *should*, I know it's time for an extra dose of self-compassion. Sometimes, I'll even give myself a hug or a little pat as if to say, *Dude, I totally get it. This is something you've been carrying around for decades. It's not easy to shake, and I'm with you on this.*

I also give myself a little slack, especially when I need it most. Self-compassion paves the way to recognizing that none of us will ever be perfect, no matter how hard we try. More than that, it's about making peace with that fact and truly embracing it. We are perfectly imperfect!

Developing self-compassion begins with the work we do while practicing mindfulness meditation. For many people, beginning to meditate can feel like an excruciating experience. You're sitting still, often on a mat or a cushion, possibly expecting to have a transcendent experience.

Instead, your brain flits between your grocery list, an insensitive comment made by a coworker, and a disagreement you had with your partner or spouse. The more you try to focus, the more emotions work their way to the surface, filling you with frustration or sadness.

Meanwhile, your left leg feels like it's about to fall asleep, and there's an itch on the tip of your nose that you're just dying to scratch.

Building self-compassion is about learning to take all of these experiences and sensations in stride. When I'm teaching mindfulness meditation, I ask participants to practice distinguishing between the types and severity of emotion. If what they're experiencing is anger or embarrassment triggered by typical life experiences, I encourage them to stay with those feelings.

If, however, the emotions coming to the surface are the result of trauma or abuse (a past sexual assault, a current abusive relationship, or a recent serious accident or natural disaster), it's usually best to put off a new meditation practice until you've developed a relationship with a therapist or mental healthcare provider who can help guide and frame your mindfulness journey in a productive and supportive way.

Without that kind of guidance, meditation can actually do harm and lead to panic attacks or an overwhelming sense of anxiety. For those reasons alone, refraining from meditation until you've had a chance to reconcile with your trauma may be the best way to show true self-compassion.

As for those annoying itches, you're just dying to scratch and the tingling sensation in your feet after sitting cross-legged for a stretch of time? I always like to remind my students that a valuable part of the meditation practice is our ability to sit quietly and unmoving. Sitting still is a powerful exercise for building our mindfulness muscles.

The trick is to invite ourselves to observe physical sensations and be present with them. Mindfulness asks that we simply notice them, whether it's a feeling of hot, cold, sharp, throbbing, tickle, or sore, and that we resist the sometimes constant temptation to fix, change, or improve. That said, if those sensations begin to feel unbearable, go ahead and care for yourself.

Remember, there is no right and wrong here. Instead, we're working to build the mindfulness muscle. Giving yourself permission to scratch an itch or think a negative thought without judgment is part of that workout routine. And the added bonus is that each time we return our minds to the act of meditation, we are making our muscles that much stronger.

Finally, keep in mind that self-compassion is most beneficial when it stems from a desire to be authentic, particularly in our relationships. Just as in my women's group talking circle, self-compassion, through our empathetic presence, allows us to be supportive of people going through their own challenges.

May You Know Peace: Developing Compassion for Others

Whether it's listening in stillness to a heartbroken friend or bringing a hot meal to an aging neighbor, compassion for others can take many forms. The more we practice self-compassion and learn to sit with our discomfort, the easier it becomes to demonstrate that same loving kindness to others. That's not to say it's always, or even ever, going to be easy.

For me, one of the most challenging times to demonstrate compassion for others is after someone has passed away. Even after all my years of training and mindfulness practice, I still struggle to find the right words for a grieving friend or loved one. Knowing there's nothing you can say to make them feel better or alleviate their deep grief has always left me feeling awkward and even helpless.

Standing in a long receiving line at a wake or memorial, I'll often find myself at a loss for words. It's then I remember my own moments of profound grief and how a simple hug or touch of the hand was often more meaningful than any words of comfort. Oftentimes, just bearing witness is the best consolation we can offer.

For many of us, compassion for friends and loved ones comes fairly easily. What's really challenging is finding open-heartedness for the difficult people in our lives—whether it's a narcissistic family member, a toxic supervisor, or even just an inconsiderate neighbor.

I've always found a saying often attributed to Lao Tzu to be particularly helpful in situations like these. The saying goes, *You can always trust a snake to be a snake.* In other words, you can always trust people to be exactly as they are.

Knowing that someone is going to follow their own value system to the best of their ability helps give us a sense of equanimity for others. It also allows us to create healthy boundaries that can prevent us from being stung by a viper who's just doing what vipers do.

When we are willing to accept people for who they really are, we give ourselves the opportunity to choose the individuals we want to surround ourselves with. It puts the responsibility of understanding and accepting on us, and it prevents us from trying to change them or force them into our own value system. It also helps avoid disappointment and heartache.

Several years ago, I was the life coach to a young man whom my husband had the opportunity to hire. Life coaches are bound by the same kinds of confidentiality as therapists, so when my husband approached me about the prospect of hiring this young man, I couldn't offer much of anything by way of a recommendation for or against his candidacy.

"Do your due diligence," I advised my husband instead.

In the end, my husband decided to hire the young man. He didn't work out, as I had well suspected he wouldn't. And my husband was furious.

"Why didn't you tell me he wasn't going to be a good hire?" he demanded.

I explained again that, as a coach, I couldn't reveal any personal information about my client. And I reminded my husband it was his responsibility to really dig into the young man's application and qualifications.

That was undoubtedly a painful lesson for my husband, but it's one we all can learn from. It's not helpful for any of us to hold other people to our personal values and expectations. Rather, it's our responsibility to discover their true characters and act to protect ourselves and to preserve the principles that are important to us.

Doing so is the best way to show compassion both for ourselves and others. Why? Because we're letting a snake be exactly as it is. We're allowing the snake to live its life exactly as it chooses. We're not encouraging it; we're not condemning it. We're not judging the snake as good or bad. We're simply noticing its characteristics as a snake and acting accordingly.

If it's a rattlesnake, that may mean giving it a very wide berth as we safely walk around it. And from ten feet away, we can still admire what is beautiful and strong about the snake. We just don't have to engage it and risk a venomous bite.

Far too often, we heap our expectations on others and then are deeply disappointed when they fail to live up to these expectations. Identifying these expectations and noticing when we project them onto people is an important first step in building compassion. Paying attention to those feelings of disappointment, along with when and how they rise, can also help us gain a better understanding of the habituated assumptions about human nature that we make on a regular basis.

We all have the capacity for lifelong learning and growth. I, personally, am continuing to learn about myself and human nature, gaining new insights into the principles that are important to me and the ways in which I am living or not living within those principles. With each lesson, I can then recalibrate and choose different actions based on what I learn, particularly where my most important relationships are concerned.

Recently, my husband and I entered into our first joint business venture—a property management company focusing on revitalizing urban commercial and residential properties. Between us, we have decades of experience as entrepreneurs; however, we'd never before worked together on a business project.

It didn't take long before I realized it wasn't a good fit. We both have strong personalities, along with a very strong desire to be in charge. I knew there was no way we could continue as co-leaders of our new business without it wreaking havoc on our marriage.

I made the decision to remove myself from a leadership role in the company. In hindsight, I realize I had made quite a few assumptions about how that business partnership would work and what role we would both play, and I didn't take into account our very different business styles.

Knowing neither he nor I were going to alter our leadership style, absenting myself from the company was the best decision for both of us.

I highly doubt I would have been able to make that decision (and protect my very wonderful marriage) had it not been for my mindfulness practice. In the past, I would have been positive that my leadership style was the "right" style, and my actions and responses would have reflected my growing frustration.

Because I was able to identify those responses and their causes early, I had the cool-headedness I needed to make a decision that was best for both of us. I established boundaries that were right for me, and I acted in a way that reflected my values.

So, how can we use mindfulness to build greater compassion for others? One of my favorite methods is the loving kindness meditation. Basically, this practice involves repeating a three-part mantra that begins with *may I be well, may I be happy, may I know peace.* From there, the meditation widens outward to *may you be well, may you be happy, may you know peace,* and finally, *may all beings be well, may all beings be happy, may all beings know peace.*

Laboratory studies have shown that reciting the loving kindness meditation encourages a very specific activity in the brain that enhances positive emotions and our capacity for empathy.[1] Researchers have also found this practice not only reduced stress-induced behaviors and immune responses, but it also increased the number of positive emotions test subjects experienced in a day. This, in turn, increased their sense of purpose and interpersonal connections while also improving their overall happiness and sense of satisfaction in life.[2]

I once had cause to share these benefits with a beloved client of mine. She was a regular attendee of my classes and seminars, and over time, we became friends. One day, she came to me with a challenge: a coworker was driving her crazy, she said, and she wanted some mindfulness tools to help her manage the situation. I suggested she practice the loving kindness meditation the next time she was with her co-worker.

"Just repeat it in your head," I told her, "and really embody the sentiment."

I also told her to focus on wishing herself peace and happiness and to imagine what it would look and feel like to experience those things. I encouraged her to do the same when she thought about her coworker.

"Really picture her in your mind's eye," I told my client. "Imagine yourself sending that energy out to her."

And, of course, I suggested she do the same visualization with the whole world when she reached that segment of the meditation. I told her that, if nothing else, *the mantra will definitely make you feel better.* She agreed to give it a shot.

As time went on, I completely forgot about the conversation. A few weeks later, my client attended one of my new classes. She approached me, just beaming.

"Oh my gosh," she said. "I just have to tell you that the thing you told me to do totally worked!"

I struggled to remember what piece of wisdom I'd offered that might have made such a difference, and I couldn't recall a thing.

"You're going to have to remind me," I eventually responded.

She went on and on about the loving kindness mantra and the magic it had performed.

"It's changed everything with my coworker," my client concluded.

I told her I was so glad to hear that. I also recommended she consider the possibility that there hadn't been any magic involved. Instead, the mantra helped to change my client's energy. It changed how she was relating to her coworker, and that shift had the power to change her coworker's response. Knowing this didn't make the experience any less powerful; it simply located the catalyst of that transformation where it belonged: with my client's intention for the encounter and within her own mind.

That's the power of mindfulness.

And, Finally, a Word on the Importance of Gratitude

A few years ago, I committed to writing a series of daily blog posts detailing what I felt grateful for each day. I managed to publish exactly one post before I became so annoyed by the whole social media thing that I gave up. That decision to stop was accompanied by guilt and shame: I felt like a quitter.

But one of the real benefits of mindfulness is we learn to live life in the moment, without wishing for something else. In this case, I was able to recognize that no one had imposed this blog project on me except for myself, and no one outside of myself really cared whether I saw it through or not.

That moment of self-compassion was a real milestone for me. For most of my life, I'd battled with perfectionism and a preoccupation with what I thought other people were thinking about me. I'd been great at showing compassion for others and had rarely stopped to give the same consideration to myself. Offering myself a little grace where that blog project was concerned was one of the greatest gifts I could give.

Surrendering those blog posts also allowed me to realize just how often I feel moments of gratitude on any given day. I don't need a grand gesture like a social media publication to acknowledge them; just a quiet moment of thanks can more than do the job. And that, I soon realized, is really what the mindfulness life is all about.

Medical researchers have now proven that higher levels of gratitude produce greater capacities for compassionate love and empathy. Not only that, but we now know that gratitude and compassion exist in the same part of our brains. They are fundamentally connected at the most molecular level.

The more we practice gratitude, the more opportunities we have for greater compassion and love. Knowing that, we would all benefit from some more gratitude in our lives.

Just as mindfulness is a muscle, so, too, is gratitude. Whether it's chasing a flock of geese in memory of a dearly departed dog or taking the time to register how our body responds to a beautiful sunset, moments of gratitude can be mindfulness practice at its very best.

When we experience gratitude, what we're really feeling is connection: to our most cherished loved ones (both two- and four-legged), to the ground beneath our feet, to the air we breathe. In those moments, we recognize we are not separate from the world around us but rather a part of this big, beautiful, greater whole.

By using our mindfulness training to choose gratitude, we are making a choice to be present in a moment and to accept it for what it is. We are choosing to celebrate the sunlight as it illuminates the tips of trees or to revel in the smell of a newborn baby's head.

That act of noticing allows us to remove our filters and experience the very essence of life. It allows us to see the beauty and joy in everyday moments and to release ourselves from the shackles of preexisting biases and prejudice. Just as importantly, it is an invitation to new possibilities: to be vulnerable, to shed the protective layers we've built year after year, to experience the world in new and more refreshing ways.

A mindfulness practice allows us to choose gratitude. It opens us up to a deep state of awareness that allows us to know our sensations and emotions. It builds connections between us and everything we see, smell, taste, touch, hear, and think.

There's been a lot of talk about love languages in recent years. And while the concept may have become something of a cliché for some, it's worth considering as you begin your mindfulness path.

Find your love language, and don't be afraid to communicate with yourself in that way. Maybe it's giving yourself a hug after a difficult meeting or buying yourself a bouquet of flowers at a farmstand. Perhaps it's daily statements of affirmation or taking the time to plant some native pollinators in your yard.

If you take anything away from this book, I sincerely hope it is a commitment to build a greater connection with yourself—to embrace yourself with the same compassion you would offer a dear friend.

The practice of mindfulness does not exist in our brains alone but rather in every cell of our body. It's there to enjoy in each physical sensation, each feeling and thought, no matter how fleeting. By inviting yourself to practice mindfulness and to begin noticing the world around you, you are inviting yourself to experience real gratitude for the warmth of the sun on your skin and the brush of wind on your face.

Chapter 8 Takeaways

- The root of the word *compassion* comes from the Latin for "suffering together." By practicing compassion, we are bearing witness to suffering, whether it is ours or other people's.

- A capacity for compassion is an important part of the mindfulness journey. To practice compassion, we must first learn to sit with uncomfortable emotions and feelings without attempting to mask or judge them.

- When practicing self-compassion, the first step is to acknowledge our present state without judgment or assigning value. In these moments, it's helpful to remember we are all perfectly imperfect—even great mindfulness practitioners like the Dalai Lama.

- Practicing self-compassion makes it easier for us to feel and demonstrate compassion for others. This, in turn, allows us to practice greater loving kindness as well.

- One way to develop compassion and loving kindness for others is to remember you can always trust people to behave exactly as they are. Accepting that their value systems and behaviors may be contrary to ours can save a lot of disappointment, rejection, and futile attempts to change other people. It can also help us establish healthy boundaries.

- Practicing loving kindness develops our brain and its capacity for both empathy and positive emotions. It also reduces stress and improves our overall well-being.

- Gratitude reinforces our connection to others and to the universe as a whole. It reminds us we are an integral part of complex webs and ecosystems that are both literal and metaphoric.

- A sense of gratitude also allows us to enjoy everyday beauty and joy, even in seemingly mundane or ordinary moments. Doing so increases our happiness and overall sense of well-being.

- Researchers now also understand that compassion and gratitude are linked within the brain. The more we practice gratitude, the greater capacity we have for compassion and love.

Chapter 8 Exercises

Formal Mindfulness Practice

Meditation on Gratitude and Joy

Adapted from Jack Kornfield and Norman Zoketsu Fisher, *The Art of Forgiveness, Lovingkindness, and Peace*

Let yourself sit quietly and at ease. Allow your body to be relaxed and open, your breath natural, your heart easy. Begin the practice of gratitude by feeling how year after year you have cared for your own life. Now let yourself begin to acknowledge all that has supported you in this care:

With gratitude, I remember the people, animals, plants, insects, creatures of the sky and sea, air and water, fire and earth, all whose joyful exertion blesses my life every day.

With gratitude, I remember the care and labor of a thousand generations of elders and ancestors who came before me.

I offer my gratitude for the safety and well-being I have been given.
I offer my gratitude for the blessing of this earth I have been given.
I offer my gratitude for the measure of health I have been given.
I offer my gratitude for the family and friends I have been given.
I offer my gratitude for the community I have been given.
I offer my gratitude for the teachings and lessons I have been given.
I offer my gratitude for the life I have been given.

Just as we are grateful for our blessings, so too can we be grateful for the blessings of others.

Continue to breathe gently. Bring to mind someone you care about, someone it is easy to rejoice for. Picture them and feel the natural joy you have for their well-being, for their happiness and success. With each breath, offer them your grateful, heartfelt wishes:

May you be joyful.
May your happiness increase.
May you not be separated from great happiness.
May your good fortune and the causes for your joy and happiness increase.

Sense the sympathetic joy and caring in each phrase. When you feel some degree of natural gratitude for the happiness of this loved one, extend this practice to another person you care about. Recite the same simple phrases that express your heart's intention.

Then gradually open the meditation to include neutral people, difficult people, and even enemies until you extend sympathetic joy to all beings everywhere, young and old, near and far.

Practice dwelling in joy until the deliberate effort of practice drops away and the intentions of joy blend into the natural joy of your own wise heart.

Loving Kindness Meditation

This is a formal mindfulness meditation practice that can foster and support compassion and well-being. If you adopt this practice, you may discover you find more self-compassion, ease, and joy in your relationships.

So, let's begin.

We begin by assuming a mindful posture that tells our body we're moving into a practice of deep awareness. We'll start by "finding our seat."

If you haven't already, I invite you to find a comfortable position where you can be alert yet relaxed: a quiet and peaceful place where you can practice self-compassion.

When you're ready, close your eyes or keep them open, whatever feels best for you at this moment. Gently balance your feet or your body on the floor or your bottom in the seat.

Take a deep breath in, and as you release that breath, let yourself relax. Notice where you might be holding tension and breathe into that place.

Breath in. Then, on the exhale, let that tension go.

Take another breath in and out. Take a moment to notice the ways your body moves with your breath—your inhale and your exhale. Allow yourself to remember there is nothing to fix or change. Your breath is as it is in this moment.

In cultivating compassion, I invite you to gradually let your imagination go. Think of a person close to you who loves you very much: someone from your past or present, still living or who has passed. It could be a friend, family member, or mentor.

Encourage yourself to imagine that person standing by your side, sending you their love. Possibly, you see the energy of their love moving toward you. Or you hear the hum and feel the warm wishes and love coming from that person. They are sending you wishes for your safety, well-being, and happiness.

Bring your attention to these sensations and receive their warmth, love, and compassion into yourself, repeating these words:

I am loveable. I am loved. I am perfect exactly as I am.

Take a deep breath in and out, anchoring yourself in the present moment.

Now, when you're ready, you are welcome to gently return your attention to the person metaphorically standing by your side.

I invite you to project and send the love you sense and feel back to that person. Send all your love and warm wishes to that person, and repeat these words:

You are loveable. You are loved. You are perfect exactly as you are.

At your own pace, expand your awareness to include your friends, family, community, and the world. Picture them on the ball of a globe in front of you.

And if you wish to, send warm wishes to all living beings on the globe who, like you, want to be healthy and happy. Repeat these words:

May all beings be well. May all beings be happy. May all beings know peace.

Take a deep breath in, anchoring yourself in this moment. Slowly exhale. Take another breath in, noticing the state of your mind and how you feel.

Wiggle your fingers and your toes, sending gratitude to your body for the ways it supports your movement and rest in the world.

And, when you're ready, open your eyes.

Informal Mindfulness Practice

What follows are some of my favorite mantras, which can be said any time you (or someone you love) would benefit from a little extra compassion. Feel free to develop your own as well. As you become accustomed to reciting mantras, you might consider writing them on Post-it Notes and leaving them in key places, such as on your refrigerator, your bathroom mirror, your computer, or the dashboard of your car.

May I (you, all beings) be well.

May I (you, all beings) be happy.
May I (you, all beings) know peace.

May my mind be at ease.
May I be at ease with my mind.

May my body be at ease.
May I be at ease with my body.

Breathing in, I calm my body and mind.
Breathing out, I smile.

Now I'm breathing in.
And now I'm breathing out.

I'm inhaling an affirmative word (love, light, joy, healing, health, forgiveness, etc.) for me.
I'm exhaling an affirmative word (whatever feels right to you) for you.

Conclusion

The time will come
when, with elation
you will greet yourself arriving
at your own door, in your own mirror
and each will smile at the other's welcome.
— Derek Walcott, "Love After Love"

For so many of us, these are difficult times. Whether it's news of global catastrophes like climate change, famine, and war, or whether it's more personal challenges like intimate relationships, family finances, or recognizing our own self-worth, it can feel like there is no shortage of reasons to check out from reality.

But if you take away even just one lesson from *The Right Side of Happiness*, let it be this: it's okay to feel grief, despair, anger, and doubt. Even more to the point, these emotions are a powerful—and even essential—part of being human.

By practicing mindfulness, we learn the value in holding these feelings with an open palm. We discover we have capacity to experience these emotions and that there is insight and growth to be had in them. And, once these feelings have the space they need to manifest, they dissipate like fog on a cool September morning, revealing the warm sun of insight and newfound joy.

By reading the concepts shared in the preceding chapters and incorporating some of the practices I've offered, you have already taken a significant step towards cultivating a mindset that fosters awareness, self-compassion, and genuine happiness.

As you continue in this journey, remember the exercises provided here are tools that will support and guide you throughout your lifelong practice, reminding you that even momentary pauses for mindfulness practice can lead to profound changes in your daily life.

And remember: a mindfulness journey is not about achieving perfection. Instead, it's about embracing our perceived imperfections with grace and curiosity. It's about recognizing the intricate connections between our thoughts, emotions, and physical sensations and using that awareness to make choices aligned with our deepest values.

Whether it's the simple act of choosing a healthy breakfast or the complex process of navigating life's challenges, mindfulness empowers us to live with greater clarity and purpose.

Happiness is not a destination. It's a journey of continuous discovery. It's about leaning into and embracing experiences as they come our way instead of judging or resisting them. It's about learning to trust in our own capacities and inherent self-worth.

And make no mistake about it: this process has the power not just to revolutionize how we see ourselves but also to change the world. With each mindful moment, you're not only improving your own well-being; you are also making the planet a more compassionate and conscious place, one based on radical acceptance, empathy, and equanimity.

So, as you close this book and step back into the rhythm of your daily life, remember the right side of happiness is always within reach—one mindful breath at a time.

Thank you so much for joining me on this journey!

Endnotes

Chapter 1

[1] "Jon Kabat-Zinn: Defining Mindfulness," Mindful, September 23, 2024, https://www.mindful.org/jon-kabat-zinn-defining-mindfulness/.

[2] Zhang, Dexing, et al. "Mindfulness-based interventions: an overall review." *British Medical Bulletin*, Volume 138, Issue 1, June 2021, Pages 41–57. This study builds upon a similar one published in 2011, which traced empirical studies demonstrating the positive impacts of mindfulness on psychological health as well as laboratory-based research on the immediate emotional and behavioral benefits derived from even brief mindfulness-based activities (Smoski, Moira J. et al, "The Effects of Mindfulness on Psychological Health: A Review of Empirical Studies." *Clin Psychol Rev.* 2011 31:6. 1041-1056.)

Chapter 2

[1] Brouwer, Ambroos, et al. "Age biases the judgment rather than the perception of an ambiguous figure." *Nature.* 11 (April 2021). https://www.nature.com/articles/s41598-021-88139-1?fromPaywallRec=false

[2] *The Miracle of Mindfulness*. Boston: Beacon Press, 1976.

[3] Lazar, Sara W. "Meditation Experience Is Associated with Increased Cortical Thickness." *Neuroreport*. 16:17 (Nov 2005). 1893-1897.

[4] Jha, Amishi P et al. "Examining the protective effects of mindfulness training on working memory capacity and affective experience." *Emotion (Washington, D.C.)* vol. 10,1 (2010): 54-64.

[5] Holzel, Britta K. et al. "Differential Engagement of Anterior Cingulate and Adjacent Medial Frontal Cortex in Adept Meditators and Non-Meditators." *Neuroscience Letters*. 421:1 (June 2007). 16-21.

[6] Brown, Kirk Warren, and Richard M Ryan. "The benefits of being present: mindfulness and its role in psychological well-being." *Journal of personality and social psychology* vol. 84,4 (2003): 822-48. doi:10.1037/0022-3514.84.4.822

[7] *Ibid.*

[8] Keng, Shian-Ling et al. "Effects of mindfulness on psychological health: a review of empirical studies." *Clinical psychology review* vol. 31,6 (2011): 1041-56.

[9] Danzico, Matt. "Brains of Buddhist Monks Scanned in Meditation Study." *BBC*. 24 April 2011. https://www.bbc.com/news/world-us-canada-12661646

Chapter 3

[1] This work actually began in the 18th century with the pioneering research of English neurologist Thomas Willis. For a fascinating account of how that early research eventually led to the late 20th-century discovery of brain neurons in the heart, consider Neil Herring and David J. Paterson's "The Heart's Little Brain: Shedding New Light and Clarity on the 'Black Box.'" *Circulation Research*. 2021. 128:1297-1299. Since then, a group of medical scholars at Thomas Jefferson University have completed extensive studies of the relationship between heart and brain neurons and their exchange of information.

[2] Duke University neuroscientist Diego Bohórquez pioneered this work. His first publication on the subject was Kaelberer, M. M., & Bohórquez, D. V. (2018). Where the gut meets the brain. *Brain Res*, *1693*(Pt B), 127. https://doi.org/10.1016/j.brainres.2018.04.039. Since then, he's proven just how connected our guts and brains truly are.

[3] Carabotti M, Scirocco A, Maselli MA, Severi C. "The gut-brain axis: interactions between enteric microbiota, central and enteric nervous systems." *Ann Gastroenterol.* 2015 Apr-Jun;28(2):203-209.

[4] M Hasan Mohajeri, Giorgio La Fata, Robert E Steinert, Peter Weber. "Relationship between the gut microbiome and brain function." *Nutrition Reviews*, Volume 76, Issue 7, July 2018, Pages 481–496

[5] Robinson, Bryan E. "The 90-Second Rule That Builds Self-Control." *Psychology Today.* April 2020.

Chapter 4

[1] Chu B, Marwaha K, Sanvictores T, et al. *Physiology, Stress Reaction.* [Updated 2022 Sep 12]. In: StatPearls [Internet]. Treasure Island (FL): StatPearls Publishing; 2023 Jan-. Available from: https://www.ncbi.nlm.nih.gov/books/NBK541120/

[2] Pretty J, Rogerson M, Barton J. Green Mind Theory: How Brain-Body-Behaviour Links into Natural and Social Environments for Healthy Habits. Int J Environ Res Public Health. 2017 Jun 30;14(7):706. doi: 10.3390/ijerph14070706. PMID: 28665327; PMCID: PMC5551144.

[3] See Graziano, Michael. *Rethinking Consciousness: A Scientific Theory of Subjective Experience.* New York: W.W. Norton, 2019. Rosenthal, David. *Consciousness and Mind. New York: Clarendon Press, 2005.*

[4] Jensen, Frances E. and Nutt, Amy Ellis. *The Teenage Brain: A Neuroscientist's Survival Guide to Raising Adolescents and Young Adults.* New York: Harper, 2015.

[5] Brandt, Lasse et al. "The effects of social isolation stress and discrimination on mental health." *Translational psychiatry* vol. 12,1 398. 21 Sep. 2022, doi:10.1038/s41398-022-02178-4

[6] Kulshreshtha A, Alonso A, McClure LA, Hajjar I, Manly JJ, Judd S. Association of Stress With Cognitive Function Among Older Black and White US Adults. *JAMA Netw Open.* 2023;6(3):e231860.

[7] Scott, Stacey B et al. "The Effects of Stress on Cognitive Aging, Physiology and Emotion (ESCAPE) Project." *BMC psychiatry* vol. 15 146. 3 Jul. 2015, doi:10.1186/s12888-015-0497-7

[8] Bartlett, Larissa et al. "Mindfulness Is Associated With Lower Stress and Higher Work Engagement in a Large Sample of MOOC Participants. *Frontiers in Psychology.* 12 (2021).

[9] Researchers have found a wide spectrum of bodily responses to trauma, ranging from poor body image and disordered eating to disassociation and somatization, or the expression of psychological and emotional stress as physical ailments, including severe headaches, chest pains, and nausea. See, for instance: Brewerton, Timothy D. "Stress, Trauma, and Adversity as Risk Factors in the Development of Eating Disorders." *The Wiley Handbook of Eating Disorders, Assessment, Prevention, Treatment, Policy, and Future Directions.* Eds. Linda Smolak and Michael P. Levine. New York: John Wiley & Sons, Ltd. 2015. Freysteinson, et al. "Body Image Perceptions of Women Veterans with Military Sexual Trauma." *Issues in Mental Health Nursing.* 39:8. 623-632. Sack et al, "Association of Nonsexual and Sexual Traumatizations with Body Image and Psychosomatic Symptoms in Psychosomatic Outpatients," *General Hospital Psychiatry.* 2010. 32:3 (315-320).

[10] One of the most influential studies on this subject was Yehuda et al's "Holocaust Exposure Induced Intergenerational Effects of FKBP5 Methylation." *Biological Psychiatry.* 2015. 80:5. 372-380. Since then, other researchers have further proved the different ways in which a parent's biology can not only change their children's biology, but also those of future generations as well. For more on that, see Andrew Curry's "Parents' Emotional Trauma May Change Their Children's Biology. Studies in Mice Show How." *Science.* 18 July 2019. https://www.science.org/content/article/parents-emotional-trauma-may-change-their-children-s-biology-studies-mice-show-how. Accessed 17 September 2023.

[11] Brom D, Stokar Y, Lawi C, Nuriel-Porat V, Ziv Y, Lerner K, Ross G. Somatic Experiencing for Posttraumatic Stress Disorder: A Randomized Controlled Outcome Study. *J Trauma Stress.* 2017. 30(3):304-312

[12] E. Oren, R. Solomon, "EMDR therapy: An overview of its development and mechanisms of action." *European Review of Applied Psychology.* 2012. 62:4. 197-203.

[13] Dietrich, Z. C., Joye, S. W., & Garcia, J. A. (2015). Natural Medicine: Wilderness Experience Outcomes for Combat Veterans. *Journal of Experiential Education, 38*(4), 394–406.

[14] Gaffney, Isabelle Ong, et al. Yoga and the Healing of Interpersonal Trauma: A Qualitative Meta-Analysis. *International Journal of Yoga Therapy.* No. 33 (2023).

Chapter 5

[1] Regan MA, Strayer DL. "Towards an understanding of driver inattention: taxonomy and theory." *Ann Adv Automot Med.* 2014;58:5-14. PMID: 24776222; PMCID: PMC4001671.

[2] Shermer, Michael. *The Believing Brain: From Ghosts and Gods to Politics and Conspiracies — How We Construct Beliefs and Reinforce Them as Truths.* New York: Times Books, 2011.

[3] Hanson, Rick. "Positive Neuroplasticity: The Neuroscience of Mindfulness." *Advances in Contemplative Psychotherapy: Accelerating Personal and Social Transformation.* Eds: Joseph Loizzo, et al. New York: Routledge, 2023.

Chapter 6

[1] Juan A. Arias, et al. "The Neuroscience of Sadness: A Multidisciplinary Synthesis and Collaborative Review." *Neuroscience & Biobehavioral Reviews,* (2020). 11. 199-228.

[2] These particular values are influenced by Don Miguel Ruiz's *The Four Agreements: A Practical Guide to Personal Freedom,* which I've also used to establish the core values of my company, Mind Body Align.

Chapter 7

[1] Kerai, Alex. "Cell Phone Usage Statistics: Mornings Are for Notifications." July 2023. https://www.reviews.org/mobile/cell-phone-addiction/. Accessed: 01 May 2024.

Chapter 8

[1] Antoine Lutz et al, "Regulation of the Neural Circuitry of Emotion by Compassion Meditation: Effects of Meditative Expertise." *PLoS.* March 2008. 26;3(3):e1897.

[2] Thaddeus W.W. Pace et al. "Effect of Compassion Meditation on Neuroendocrine, Innate Immune and Behavioral Responses to Psychosocial Stress." *Psychoneuroendocrinology.* Jan 2009. 34(1). 87-98. Also, Frederickson, Barbara L. "Open Hearts Build Lives:

Positive Emotions, Induced Through Loving-Kindness Meditation, Build Consequential Personal Resources." *J Pers Soc Psychol.* Nov 2008. (95)5. 1045-1062.

Acknowledgments

I'm deeply grateful to all the incredible people who have supported me in the journey of writing *The Right Side of Happiness*. First and foremost, to my husband, Carl—my partner and mentor, a man who embodies mindfulness effortlessly. Your wisdom, guidance, and unwavering belief in the power of a mindful life have kept me grounded and focused when distractions threatened to pull me off course. You inspire me every day.

To my sister Julie, thank you for your deep compassion and the wealth of knowledge you bring from your work in elementary education. Your trust in our shared mission and your leadership in bringing Mind Body Align to schools has been invaluable.

And to my sister Terise, your brilliance in PR, your editorial eye, and your sharp, strategic thinking have been a beacon of clarity in this process. Your support means the world to me.

To Marcy Bemiller, my best friend since 6th grade, your influence shows up throughout this book. I'm grateful for you!

I also want to express my heartfelt thanks to the Mind Body Align team members who continually encouraged and supported me in the writing of this book: Jennifer Blue, Diane Hostettler, Mary Kennard, and Linda Snyder.

To the early readers, Sandy Abrams, author of *Breathe to Succeed*; Kristoffer Carter, author of *Permission to Glow*; Dr. Benjamin Hardy, author of *Be Your Future Self Now* and *10X is Easier than 2X*; and Due Quach, author of *Calm Clarity*—your feedback made this book better. I am immensely grateful for your time, insights, and wisdom.

I would also like to thank Dr. Brené Brown, Diana Brown, Grace Cirocco, Sally Gesouras, and Jack Kornfield for allowing me to use their stories or intellectual property in this book. Your contributions have enriched the depth and authenticity of this work.

I had a lot of help in the writing and editing of this book. Katherine Miles, author of *Trailed: One Woman's Quest to Solve The Shenandoah Murders*. You were my coach, therapist, editor, and friend. You have left your mark throughout this book, making it better, and me a better writer. And thank you also to Chris Murray for your insightful book review and editing.

To the Coffee Talk Ladies, Mindfulness 101 veterans, friends, and everyone who believed in me and this vision—thank you. This book is a reflection of the love, encouragement, and wisdom you have all so generously given.

About the Author

Annamarie Fernyak is the Founder and CEO of the mindful education company, Mind Body Align LLC. She is an award-winning community leader who lives and works to make life better in downtown Mansfield, Ohio. She is the author of *The Right Side of Happiness* and is an educator, speaker, podcast guest, and writer on building resilience and living mindfully in the present moment as the path to a life of true happiness and contentment. Mind Body Align teaches hundreds of students and educators each year how to pay focused attention, practice kindness, and share gratitude.

Annamarie is the co-author of a 16-book series for children and is the vision behind the main character, Tia, a butterfly, and Dwight, a grasshopper, two of the delightful inhabitants of a special garden labyrinth. These books teach children skills of self-regulation, how to navigate disagreement, to manage anxiety, and more. This series is set in a real-life labyrinth at Annamarie's farm in Lucas.

Annamarie is often found traveling and camping in her Airstream trailer. Connect with Annamarie on Instagram @MindfullyAnnamarie.

STAY CONNECTED

Continue your journey of growth and mindfulness with me. Stay updated on new articles, tips, and insights by subscribing at AnnamarieFernyak.com.

TAKE THE NEXT STEP ON YOUR JOURNEY TO HAPPINESS

DOWNLOAD FREE MINDFULNESS MEDITATIONS AND EXERCISES THAT WILL SUPPORT YOUR WELL-BEING.

AnnamarieFernyak.com

LET'S SHARE THE MESSAGE OF MINDFUL LIVING TOGETHER!

I'M AVAILABLE TO APPEAR ON YOUR PODCAST AND INSPIRE YOUR AUDIENCE WITH PRACTICAL TOOLS FOR HAPPINESS AND MINDFULNESS.

AnnamarieFernyak.com

www.ingramcontent.com/pod-product-compliance
Lightning Source LLC
LaVergne TN
LVHW021315080125
800709LV00031B/329/J